1500 Interesti

Facts for Kids

A Fascinating Collection of the Interesting, Random and Awesome Facts for Curious Kids and Their Families!

<u>*Johnny Tiger*</u>

FACTS FOR ANIMAL LOVERS

1. The brain of the ostrich is smaller than its eye.

2. Koala bear's fingerprints are identical to a human's.

3. The trunk is used for drinking, smelling, eating, touching, and communicating.

4. Armadillos are able to walk underwater.

5. Wild lions usually do not kill more than 20 times a year.

6. Some favorite activities include swimming, bathing, and playing in water.

7. Scientists think that the incident that led to the extinction could have been a huge asteroid impact or volcanic eruption, which might have masked sunlight and altered the ecosystem of the Earth dramatically.

8. Elephants are the biggest mammals found on land.

9. Most plant eaters used natural weapons to help fight carnivores like the Allosaurus or Spinosaurus. Sources of this include the Stegosaurus spikes on the tail and the three horns on the front of the head shield of the Triceratops.

10. Some dinosaurs aged to be over 100 years old.

11. Emperor penguins, other than humans, are the only warm-blooded species to remain on Antarctica in winter.

12. Elephants love to use their trunk as a shower to spray themselves and others with water.

13. Toads will only eat living things.

14. It is impossible for a kangaroo to walk backwards.

15. Emus are not able to walk backward.

16. When they listen to music, most cows produce more milk.

17. The skin and fur of the tiger are both striped.

18. A paleontologist researches dinosaurs.

19. A male calf stays with the herd until he is around fifteen. Then, like most bull elephants, he leaves and lives alone.

20. Cows and horses sleep in an upright position.

21. Elephants are the only creatures to mourn the dead, apart from humans.

22. The longest poisonous snake is the King Cobra, which can grow to more than 4 meters (13 feet).

23. The fastest speed of a cheetah is 114 km/h (70 mph).

24. Elephants are very expressive–they cry when they are angry, and when they are happy they squeak and trumpet.

25. Elephants can sing by using an ultrasound rumble so low that humans cannot hear it. They use it to keep the herd together, and to find mates.

26. Chameleons can simultaneously move their eyes in two directions. In under a minute, Komodo dragons will eat five pounds of meat. They reserve any additional fat they eat in their tails.

27. A pet hamster on a wheel can run up to 8 miles in a night.

28. While Polar Bears have white, fluffy fur, they in fact have black skin.

29. Camels have three eyelids to shield their eyes from blowing sand.

30. Crocodiles by the banks of the Nile river are accountable for over 1000 deaths per annum.

31. The tongue of a chameleon is about as long as its body, but it can capture its prey in a split second.

32. An ostrich can run faster than a horse.

Spotted hyenas can eat bones and skin.

33. Only toads that are male can croak.

34. Scientists have found out that the dinosaur theropod community, which includes the T-Rex, are the birds' ancestors.

35. The slimmest of all red meats is ostrich meat.

36. Frogs ingest most of the moisture they need through their skin, instead of swallowing it.

37. An elephant never forgets.

38. The lion's roar can be heard up to 5km away and is the loudest of all the big cats.

39. While pandas may eat fish or small animals at times, bamboo accounts for 99% of their food.

40. A hippopotamus can outrun a human.

41. The nearest living relatives of hippos are marine animals like whales, dolphins, and marshes.

42. Apart from zoos, penguins naturally only occur in the Southern hemisphere.

43. The mature bison is North America's biggest land mammal.

44. Giraffes are not able to cough.

The smallest color or design change will help a plant or animal grow, survive and reproduce better in the wild. This is referred to as natural selection.

45. It takes less than 3 minutes for a camel to consume 94 liters (25 gallons) of water.

46. The Chinese giant salamander can grow to a length of 6 feet (1.8 m), it is the world's largest salamander.

47. The fur of a polar bear is colorless. The hair strand is hollow, reflecting the sun, and making it white. The skin is black, taking up the heat from the sun and keeping the bear warm.

48. In the wild, other elephants–known as aunties– will help to raise the baby. A new mother will select her aunties and they will rear the baby together.

49. Cows are able to walk up stairs, but they cannot walk down.

50. The collective noun for rhinos is a crash.

51. The collective noun for a group of kangaroos is a mob.

52. At 22 months, elephants have the longest incubation period of any land mammal.

53. Wild elephants live in herds consisting of female elephants.

54. The African Rock Python will live without food for two years.

55. While the bobcat is not often observed, it is North America's most typical wildcat.

56. When they're tickled, all primates chuckle.

57. An elephant can use his trunk to pick up a small coin, or a large tree trunk.

58. In the wild, the average polar bear can live to 17 years.

59. They suck the water up into their trunks and pump it into their mouths to drink.

60. Every day, 60 cows will produce one ton of milk.

61. Occasionally, naked mole rats are also called sand puppies.

62. A cross between a Donkey and a Zebra is called a Zonkey.

63. Some reindeer can journey over 3000 miles in one year.

64. The term dinosaur derives from the Greek meaning 'terrible lizard'. The word was created in 1842 by English paleontologist Richard Owen and was meant to refer to the enormous scale of the dinosaurs rather than their terrifying appearance.

65. Dinosaurs are thought to have lived on Earth until a mass extinction happened about 65 million years ago.

66. An elephant only sleeps around 4-5 hours in a 24 hour period.

67. Lions are not able to roar until they are 2 years old.

68. Female lions are better stalkers than males and do most of the pride's hunting.

69. The trunk of an elephant can contain more than 5 liters of water.

70. A crocodile is not able to move its tongue.

71. The herd authority is typically the oldest female, called the Matriarch.

72. A rat is able to keep swimming for three days.

73. Deer are not fond of hay.

74. To help them digest Eucalyptus leaves later in life, baby koalas are fed poo by their parents after birth.

75. Emperor penguins will survive up to 27 minutes underwater and submerge up to a depth of 500m.

76. Koalas spend about 18 hours of their day resting.

77. Elephants have a fear of dogs.

78. Elephants are so smart that they even make jokes with humans.

79. As with humans, there are seven bones in the neck of a giraffe, but they are a lot bigger.

80. Cheetahs can go from 0 to 70 km/h (43mp/h) in 3 only seconds.

81. Tame elephants will have a lifelong relationship with their mahout.

82. The African porcupine's quills are as long as three pencils.

83. Elephants adore being in water.

84. The Galápagos Islands' giant tortoise can weigh as much as 250kg (550lbs) – as much as a brown bear!

85. "Armadillo" is "little armored one" in Spanish.

86. Gorillas rest for fourteen hours a day.

87. Elephants are the largest land-based mammals on Earth.

88. There are 30,000 spikes in the typical porcupine.

89. Like humans, older monkeys can lose the hair on their heads.

90. In a single day, a platypus will consume their weight in worms.

91. Sloths can't shiver to keep warm, so holding their body temperature on rainy days is hard.

92. The wrinkle patterns on the nose of a gorilla are special to each and is referred to as a 'nose print.' Conservation staff use images and drawings of gorillas' noses to trace them.

93. We can observe from fossils that many years ago dinosaurs, woolly mammoths, and dodos existed. But we will never really know all the strange and wonderful creatures that lived before!

94. The hippopotamus has pink milk.

95. The collective noun for frogs is an army.

96. Elephants are herbivores and will only eat grass, fruit and plants.

97. Elephants are very cautious and defensive of their trunks as they are very sensitive.

98. Elephants are able to peel their own bananas, corn, and other food.

99. A jaguar is six times better able to see in the dark than a human.

100. The reindeer antlers have a velvety coat as they mature. The' velvet' will molt and chafe off when the antlers are fully grown.

101. Ordinarily, an elephant lives up to 70 years of age, as do humans.

102. The trunk of the elephant is one of the most impressive designs in nature.

103. There are two fingers at the tip of the African elephants' trunk, while the Asian elephant has one.

104. Snakes would drown if they tried to bite underwater.

105. Elephants are very fond of bananas.

106. There are three toes on each foot of a rhinoceros.

107. The milk of the camel cannot curdle.

108. It is not possible for a crocodile to extend its tongue.

109. Goats' pupils are rectangular.

110. Every day, a healthy mature elephant will consume up to 60 gallons of water–the same amount as about 275 large coke bottles.

111. Elephants use sound waves to communicate, which is inaudible to humans.

112. Some dinosaurs had tails that were longer than 13 m (45 feet).

113. Cobras in the wild can reach up to 20 years of age.

114. Wild Bactrian (two-humped) camels can consume up to 50 liters (88 pints) when they find a water source. Unlike other mammals, they can also drink saline water.

115. The largest dinosaurs were in fact herbivores rather than carnivores, such as the Brachiosaurus and Apatosaurus.

116. The Cheetah is the world's quickest land animal, measuring a maximum speed of about 113 km/ hour (70 mph).

117. To protect their muzzles when feeding, reindeer grow their facial hair longer to shield their mouths in winter.

118. Baby polar bear cubs are blind and deaf for a month after they are born.

119. An African elephant's skeleton makes up about 15% of its body weight.

120. Dinosaurs dominated the Earth for more 160 million years, from the Triassic era about 230 million years ago through the Jurassic period to the end of the Cretaceous period around 65 million years ago.

121. The collective noun for a group of foxes is a skulk.

122. Frogs take in water by absorbing it through their skin.

123.The Nile crocodile, while hunting for food, will hold its breath underwater for up to two hours.

124.The era from 250 million years ago to approximately 65 million years ago is called the Mesozoic Period. It is often called the Dinosaur Age since, during this period, most dinosaurs have evolved and died out.

125.The Megalosaurus was the first dinosaur back in 1824 to be officially named.

126.Nine-banded armadillos will always bear four indistinguishable babies.

Facts about ourselves

127. Eight percent of the population has an extra rib.

128. Your blood accounts for around 8% of your body weight.

129. Fifty-nine percent of people say they look average.

130. The biggest organ of the human body is your skin.

131. Your feet create a pint of sweat each day.

132. Humans and chimpanzees share 98.8% DNA, but they still have about 35 million distinctions.

133. In a normal lifespan, the human heart beats over three billion times.

134. You can't smell anything while you're sleeping, not even extremely unpleasant or strong smells.

135. Every year the average person takes in more than one ton of food and drink.

136. In a year, the average person has more than 1460 dreams.

137. There is about 78 percent water in the average human brain.

138. Men have 10% more red blood cells compared to women.

139. Your blood is six times as thick as water.

140. When you're cold, your fingernails grow quicker.

141. The human tongue print is as unique as a fingerprint.

142. Your nose and ears will never stop growing as long as you live.

143. There are 67 different species of bacteria in the average person's belly button.

144. Your heart beats roughly 100 000 times per day, 365 00000 times per year, and by the time you are 30, it would already have beaten more than a billion times.

145. Every four weeks, you shed a full layer of skin.

146. A person will die of complete lack of sleep earlier than of hunger (death will occur around ten days without sleep while food takes a couple of weeks).

147. Blue toothbrushes are apparently preferred to red ones.

148. Your tongue is your body's fastest recovering organ.

149. The stirrup bone in the middle ear, is the smallest bone in the human body, measuring only 2.8mm long.

150. Every second, the human body creates 2,500,000 new red blood cells.

151. A human can survive without food for about a month, but without water for only about a week.

152. The only species that blush are human beings.

153. The fastest human sense is hearing. Sound can be recognized in under 0.05 seconds.

154. Throughout your life, your nose and ears will keep growing.

155. When talking, you use 72 distinct muscles.

156. The standard temperature of your body is 37C (99F).

157. Your sense of smell is about 10 000 times more powerful than your sense of taste.

158. Scientists estimate that a trillion individual smells can be detected by the nose!

159. Not all of your taste buds are found on your tongue (10% are on your cheeks' inside).

160. Laughing reduces stress levels and builds up the immune system.

161. It is not possible for a human to lick their own elbow.

162. Scientists say between 1 PM and 2:30 PM is the perfect time to nap, as that's when we feel tired, due to a drop in body temperature.

163. The body needs about 12 hours to fully digest a meal.

164. In a single day, the mouth can make one liter of saliva.

165. When you mature, you're going to have 32 teeth.

166. You can crack a rib by sneezing too hard.

167. It takes seven minutes for most people to fall asleep.

168. On average, a person uses the toilet six times a day.

169. Your index finger, closest to your thumb, is the most tender finger.

170. Every year you shed around 4 kg skin cells

171. You can't speak, and at the same time breathe in or out.

172. Your heart and fist are around the same size.

173. Eyebrows have two functions: to protect the eyes from rain, sweat, and dirt, and also to convey emotion.

174. Approximately 70% of the adult body is water.

175. A quarter of the oxygen consumed by the human body is used by the brain.

176. The hyoid bone in your throat is not connected to any other bone in your body.

177. An average person will sleep for 25 years.

178. In the human body there are more than 10 trillion living cells.

179. The blood vessels of an adult could cross the equator of Earth four times!

180. Your left lung is about 10% smaller than your right lung.

181. There are no middle names for Japanese people.

182. 53% of all women will not go out without applying makeup.

183. The same five-fingered bone structure found in human hands, appear in lots of other animals that have paws, wings or flippers, such as lemurs and bats.

184. In the human body, the biggest internal organ is the small intestine.

185. Red blood cells are produced inside your bone marrow, and they carry oxygen around your body.

186. The longest human coma lasted 37 years.

187. 75% of the human brain consists of water, and 75% of a living tree consists of water.

188. Babies will not cry tears until they are at least a month old.

189. Sleeping can burn more calories than watching TV does.

190. Data can zoom about 400kmph along the nerves!

191. Mouthwash is used by 45% of people daily.

192. Humans have both unique fingerprints and unique tongue prints.

193. The average life span in the United States in 1900 was 47.

194. The white dots you see when you look at a bright light, are white blood cells.

195. An average of 32 million bacteria are present on every square inch of the human body.

196. If there are 23 people in a room, the chance that two them will share a birthday is 50%.

197. The human body comprises 96 000 km of blood vessels (59 650miles).

198.The number one source of arguments between couples, is money.

199.Human teeth are as solid as those of sharks.

200.California's native tribal groups spoke more than 200 separate dialects before European contact (which caused populations to decline quickly).

201.In a day, your mouth can generate about a liter of saliva!

202.Adult lungs have an area of approximately 70 square meters!

203.Every year, the average person loses 1.7 kg (1.5 pounds) of skin.

204.Melanin is the pigment that dictates the color of your skin. If you have very little you will have light skin, and if you have a large amount, you will have dark skin.

205.REM sleep, the stage that features rapid eye movement, equates to about 25% of your total sleep time and is when you have your clearest dreams.

206.The average adult blinks about 10 times per minute, while a baby blinks only once or twice.

207.There are 10 000 taste buds on the average human tongue.

208.Babies all have blue eyes at birth.

209.In a single day, you can shed as many as 100 hairs.

210.The human eye can perceive and distinguish more than 10 million colors.

211.A typical yawn lasts 6 seconds.

FACTS FOR SPACE TRAVELLERS

213. Since there is no wind to erase them, footprints and tire marks left by astronauts will stay on the moon forever.

214. Mercury's daytime temperature is more than 400 degrees Celsius, because it is very close to the sun.

215. Venus is often portrayed as a "stormy desert" full of craters and volcanoes that are very active.

216. The surface of Mars is constantly changing due to rough dust storms.

217. The sky has more stars than there are particles of sand on Earth.

218. Only one teaspoonful of a neutron star would weigh six-billion tons.

219. There are 16 hours in Neptune's day.

220. Some of the fastest meteoroids will move about 42 kilometers per second (26 miles per second) through the solar system.

221. Neptune is almost four times larger when compared to Earth.

222. The Earth's light only takes 1.255 seconds to get to the Moon.

223. Saturn is our solar system's second largest planet and is a gas giant.

224. The rocky center of Jupiter is a little larger than Earth but weighs about twenty times more.

225. Venus is encircled by clouds of mercury, hydrocarbons of ferric chloride and sulphuric acid. The most corrosive acid rain produced in our solar system is formed by these clouds.

226. Mercury does not have an atmosphere, so there is no wind or weather.

227. With a surface temperature measuring more than 450 degrees Celsius, Venus is the hottest planet in our solar system.

228. You would weigh more than twice as much on Jupiter as you would on Earth because it has a powerful magnetic field.

229. Our solar system consists of planets, moons, comets, asteroids, minor planets, dust, and gas. It all rotates around the sun.

230. On June 18, 1983, Sally Ride became the first American woman to travel in space.

231. A neutron star could rotate 600 times in a second.

232. Applesauce was the first food that astronauts consumed in space.

233. The brightest man-made location seen from space is Las Vegas.

234. Pluto had its status changed to dwarf planet in 2006.

235. When the Russian satellite Sputnik was launched in 1957, it was the first man-made object to be sent into space.

236. It takes around 10 hours for Jupiter to complete a full rotation on its axis, making it the solar system's fastest spinning planet.

237. The gravity on Mercury's surface is very weak.

238. A large dying star's collapse leads to the creation of a black hole. It has a very powerful gravitational force that pulls everything in, even light!

239. Uranus rotates on its side like a barrel, which might have been caused by a large collision early in its formation.

240. Mercury's surface is very close to that of our moon. It has a very barren, rocky surface full of craters.

241. The Solar System was created around 4.6 billion years ago.

242. Our universe has more than 125 billion galaxies. There are about 100-400 billion stars in our galaxy.

243. While Venus is the only planet in our solar system that rotates in the opposite direction to Earth, Uranus is the only one that rolls like a barrel on its side.

244. Venus' atmosphere consists largely of carbon dioxide.

245. The first hominid in space, Ham the Astrochimp, blasted off on January 31, 1961.

246. Jupiter has a number of storms raging on the surface, particularly the big red spot that is our solar system's biggest hurricane. This storm has been busy for over three hundred years.

247. In 1986, Halley's Comet was last observed in the inner Solar System. Sometime in 2061, it will be noticeable from Earth again.

248. It takes 84 Earth years for Uranus to circumvent the sun, which means that for 42 years each of its poles is in daylight and for the next 42 years it is in darkness.

249. Jupiter is surrounded by a lot of moons, four of which are larger than Pluto.

250. The thin, cold atmosphere of Jupiter becomes thicker and hotter the deeper you go down, slowly becoming a dense, dark cloud. About 1000km in, the pressure squeezes the atmosphere so hard that it becomes liquid.

251. Neptune faces the most extreme weather in our solar system.

252. The space race starts, marked by the launch of Sputnik, the first artificial orbiting satellite, by The Soviet Union.

253. There is also no water on Mercury's surface, though it is likely that under the surface there might be water.

254. You always see the same side every time you see a full moon.

255. Mars has very feeble gravity that is unable to hold on to the atmosphere very well.

256. Pluto was the smallest and most distant planet from the Sun but is now no longer a planet.

257. Because it is coated with rust-like dust, Mars is called the red planet. Even the atmosphere is a pink color, darkened by tiny dust particles from the surface.

258. Mars looks red because it has rust covering its surface.

259. It would take around 800 years to travel to Pluto on an airplane.

260. Pluto's atmosphere is made up of nitrogen, methane, and carbon monoxide.

261. Jupiter is our solar system's biggest planet. It is so massive that it can fit in more than 1300 Earths.

262. Saturn has liquid gas surrounding its small rocky center.

263. Saturn is not the only planet with rings. Other gas giants like Jupiter, Uranus and Neptune have rings as well, they are just less visible.

264. The term "astronaut" literally translates to "star sailor" in Greek.

265. Pluto is made up of rock with a very dense ice coating.

266. Venus is the only planet that rotates clockwise.

267. Saturn is encircled by a lot of moons, just like Jupiter.

268. The moon is very hot during the day (average 224 degrees Fahrenheit) but very cold at night (-243 degrees average).

269. Astronomers updated the definition of a planet in 2006. Therefore, Pluto has been demoted to a dwarf planet.

270. Saturn has storm winds dashing at 800kmph through its atmosphere.

271. Saturn is very light because it consists of more hydrogen than helium and is therefore less compact. It would float on water.

272. It rains metal on the planet Venus.

273. The sun is as big as one million Earths.

274. There are three separate types of planets; terrestrial planets (Mercury, Venus, Earth, and Mars), which are very large and rocky, gas giants (Jupiter, Saturn, Uranus, and Neptune), mainly frozen hydrogen and helium, and dwarf planets (Pluto, Ceres, and Eris), smaller planets circling the sun.

275. The moon is only 27% as large as the Earth.

276. The Sun is more than 300,000 times the size of the Earth.

277. Jupiter is big enough to fit all the planets in our solar system.

278. Neptune has thin white straggly clouds stretching all around it.

279. There is no fluid water on Venus.

280. Moons are not all dry and dusty. Jupiter's moon, Europa, is liquid and ice.

281. There will be the footsteps on the moon for 100 million years.

282. It has been found that there is opal on Mars.

283. Uranus was the first telescopically observed planet.

284. Every year, more than 500 meteorites hit the Earth.

285. The atmosphere of Uranus is primarily hydrogen, but it also has large quantities of methane. Methane absorbs red light and disperses blue light, so the planets interior is hidden from view by a blue-green methane haze.

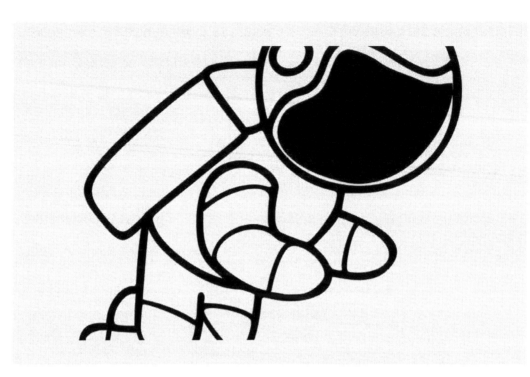

286. Because it has much less natural activity going on, the Moon looks to have more craters and marks than Earth. Earth is continuously changing its landscape through earthquakes, flooding, heat, wind, and plants developing----- on the surface.

287. Some clouds can move up to 100 mph through the sky, depending on how fast the wind is blowing.

288. Mars has a very thin, mostly carbon dioxide atmosphere. It is not as dense as that of Venus, making very cold. Temperatures range from -120 degrees Celsius in the winter nights to 25 degrees Celsius in the summer.

289. Mars has many channels, plains and canyons which in the past might have been caused by water erosion.

290. The suns' core is about 15 million C (27 million F).

291.Jupiter is surrounded by dense, colorful clouds of deadly toxic gases. The planet's fast spinning churns up the atmosphere, creating the planet's rings.

292.Neptune consists of water and has a blue hydrogen-methane atmosphere and faint rings.

293.Sound does not transmit in space.

294.Mars has a number of large volcanoes and is home to Olympus Mons, our solar system's largest volcano standing 21km high and reaching 600km across.

295.Saturn catches energy particles through its magnetic field, which causes high radiation levels.

296.Due to differences in gravity, a person normally weighing 200 pounds on earth will weigh just 76 pounds on Mars.

297.The four largest moons of Jupiter are Callisto, Europa, Ganymede, and Io.

SIMPLE FACTS FOR SMALL KIDS

299. It is impossible to lick your own elbow. No one can! Go on and try it.

300. Rubber bands break easily, but not if you put them in the fridge!

301. You can fall asleep in seven minutes; most people do.

302. A sponge can hold more cold water than it can hold hot water.

303. Giraffes cannot swim.

304. Only 11% of people on the planet are left-handed.

305. The letter that is used most in the alphabet is the letter "E."

306. The safest color for a car is white.

307. The item that most people who travel always forget is their toothbrush.

308. Eating an apple in the morning wakes you up better than drinking coffee does.

309. The most played board game in the world is Monopoly.

310. Buttermilk does not actually contain any actual butter.

311. A giraffe and a rat can survive longer without water than a camel can.

312. Statistically, women blink at least twice as much as men do.

313. The hardest natural substance is a diamond.

314. People originally played tennis using their bare hands instead of a racket to hit the ball.

315. You can only fold a piece of paper seven times.

316. Christmas trees were originally from Germany.

317. A gorilla sleeps for about 14 hours a day.

318. A butterfly will drink the tears of a turtle if they need salt.

319. The most bought ice cream flavor in America is vanilla.

320. The pea is the oldest vegetable that we know of.

321. Hens lay around 228 eggs a year.

322. The Statue of Liberty's crown has seven points.

323. Your thigh bone is stronger than concrete.

324. If a month starts on a Sunday, it will contain Friday the 13th.

325. The most common allergy in the world is cow's milk.

326. The part of your eye that contains color is called an "iris."

327. There are 22 bones in just your head.

328. An African elephant only has four teeth.

329. The first English dictionary in history was written in the year 1755.

330. The United States flag has 13 stripes that represent the 13 original states.

331. There is zero fat in carrots.

332. Soccer is the most popular sport that is played.

333. Hippopotamuses are born underwater.

334. Elephants can hold more than five liters of water in their trunks.

335. Sharks' teeth are actually harder than steel.

336. Moths do not have stomachs, and therefore, they mostly drink liquids such as nectar.

337. A grasshopper's blood is in fact white, not red.

338. Bulls are able to run faster uphill than they can run downhill.

339. Dogs sweat through their feet and their tongues.

340. The song that is sung the most is "Happy Birthday."

341. The board game of checkers is older than the board game of chess.

342. A blonde beard will grow faster than a dark-colored beard.

343. Albert Einstein, a well-known physicist, was known to have slept for ten hours a day.

344. Squirrels can live for up to nine years.

345. The word "racecar" can be spelled the same backward as it is forward.

346. A housefly only lives for about ten to 25 days.

347. Chihuahuas are the smallest dogs in the whole world.

348. The teabag was only invented in 1908; before then, people only used tea leaves.

349. A snail can go to sleep for up to three years.

350. It takes two hours to hard boil an ostrich egg.

351. People hurt their thumbs while playing ten-pin bowling more than they do any other part of their body.

352. The first country to use postage stamps was Britain.

353. The name for the side of a hammer is "cheek."

354. The name Pinocchio means "pine eyes" in Italian.

355. You should shuffle a deck of cards at least seven times before playing with them.

356. Tooth decay is the most common disease.

357. Insects will bite your foot more often than any other part of your body.

358. Our sun is about 330,330 times larger than the planet Earth.

359. The shell of an egg only makes up for 12% of its weight.

360. A squid has a total of ten tentacles.

361. A woman's heart will beat faster than a man's heart.

362. A windy day is when you are more likely to be stung by a bee than any other day.

363. You have over 10,000 taste buds living in your mouth.

364. You breathe in more air through your right lung than through your left lung.

365. "Screeched" is the longest one-syllable word in the English language.

366. A snake cannot blink at all.

367. Ants hate baby powder.

368. A rat can swim in water for up to three days before getting tired.

369. Rice paper does not actually contain any rice.

370. Sharks can never stop moving, even when they are asleep.

371. Cows will produce more milk while they are listening to music.

372. A blue whale can survive for six months without eating any food.

373. A house cat will usually have up to 18 claws.

374. There are 20,000 species of bees, but only four of them can produce honey.

375. "Save A Spider Day" is on March 14th.

376. Avocados and tomatoes are indeed fruits, not vegetables.

377. Unless you have a twin, nobody smells like you. You have your very own unique smell.

378. The Queen of England has two birthdays.

379. A slug has four noses.

380. Hippopotamuses can run faster than humans.

381. An apple is one of the few fruits that float on water.

382. The number four is the only number with the same number of letters used to write it.

383. You cannot inhale or exhale while you are talking.

384. It is impossible to hum while holding your nose closed.

385. Your fist is about the same size as your heart.

386. The board game Monopoly has been played by more than 480 million people.

387. A yawn will last for an average of about six seconds.

388. Only the male toads croak; female toads do not.

389. There are not any English words that rhyme with the word "orange."

390. Starfish do not have a brain.

391. Disney World, an amusement park in Florida, is actually bigger than about 17 countries in the world.

392. A strand of your hair can live for an average of approximately four to seven years.

393. You cannot dream of strangers. The people you see in your dreams are people that you have met once before in your life.

394. A bee has four wings, and it can beat them about 200 times per second.

395. Bananas are the most eaten fruit in America.

396. Your brain only makes up 5% of your body's total weight.

397. The elevator was invented as early as 1850 by a man named Elisha Graves Otis.

398. The first toothbrush in history was made and used in the year 1498.

RANDOM FACTS IF YOU LIKE RANDOM THINGS

PANDAS DON'T HAVE SET SLEEPING AREAS THEY JUST FALL ASLEEP WHEREVER THEY ARE.

400. It takes 120 raindrops to fill one teaspoon.

401. A woman will spend around 76 days of her life just rummaging through her handbag.

402. The record for the longest cherry pit spit was approximately 71.2 feet.

403. America has more plastic flamingos than real ones.

404. Reginald Dwight is Elton John's real name.

405. A collection of bananas is usually referred to as a "hand."

406. The sound of E.T., from the movie E.T. the Extra-Terrestrial, when he was walking, was made using jelly.

407. A python is so big that it can swallow a pig whole!

408. An average human body contains enough iron in the bloodstream to make a nail three inches tall.

409. It cost more to make the film Titanic than it cost to make the actual Titanic ship.

410. There is a book whose title is 679 words long. It is the longest title in the world for a book.

411. A salad from McDonald's is actually more fattening than a burger.

412. There are so many pieces of Lego in the world that you could give everyone at least 62 pieces each.

413. Pearls may be small, but they can actually weigh up to 13 pounds.

414. Scientists suggest that the average human will swallow about a liter of snot every day.

415. It is known that your eyesight actually improves when you are scared.

416. The fear of heights and the fear of clowns are the two most common fears on Earth.

417. There is enough carbon in your body to make around 9,000 pencils.

418. When you go up an elevator, you weigh the same, but when you are going down you weigh less.

419. We do not actually know what color the T-Rex was.

420. On average, you will unknowingly eat around 430 bugs a year.

421. In the United States, there is currently a plan on how the country can deal with a zombie apocalypse.

422. There are around six people in the world who will look exactly like you. They are known as your "doppelgänger."

423. Rabbits like to eat licorice.

424. Lobsters have clear, colorless blood, but when their blood is exposed to oxygen, it turns blue.

425. A bird needs gravity in order to swallow, so birds cannot swallow in space.

426. Spiders are not insects; they are arachnids.

427. Insects have six legs.

428. Lemon contains more sugar than a strawberry does.

429. A croissant sounds like it is French, but it was actually invented in Austria.

430. There is a type of beer in Africa that is brewed from bananas.

431. The Aztec Indians were the ones who invented popcorn.

432. Reindeer hair is like a tube because it is hollow inside.

433. The King of Hearts, in a deck of cards, is the only king of the four that does not have a mustache.

434. Unlike us and some other animals, a cat is unable to move its jaw to the side.

435. A group of frogs is referred to as an "army."

436. A large group of kangaroos is referred to as a "mob."

437. A collection of geese is referred to as a "gaggle."

438. Women purchase 96% of the candles that are sold.

439. Domesticated cats hate the smell of citrus.

440. It is forbidden to hug trees in China.

441. Mary Poppins, the film made by Disney, was filmed completely indoors.

442. A pearl will melt in vinegar.

443. Paper was originally created in China. So was the wheelbarrow.

444. You can spin a hardboiled egg, but a soft boiled or uncooked egg will not spin.

445. The name for the dot on top of the letter "I" is a "tittle."

446. The odds of you being killed by a champagne cork are higher than the odds of you being killed by a poisonous spider.

447. An ostrich actually does not bury its head in the sand when it is frightened.

448. It is only the female mosquitoes that bite; the males do not.

449. A hummingbird cannot walk at all.

450. The same company that builds the Porsche also builds tractors.

451. Iguanas are able to hold their breath underwater for up to 28 minutes.

452. The average cow will produce about 40 glasses full of milk a day.

453. Men are seven times more likely to be struck by lightning than women are.

454. Green diamonds are the rarest diamonds in the world.

455. Flies are able to launch themselves into the air backward so they can make a quick getaway.

456. A jellyfish is made up of 95% water.

457. The moon is nine times brighter when it is full than when it is a half-moon.

458. Porcupines have an average of 30,000 spikes.

459. Camels are usually born without their humps.

460. The people in Iceland drink the most Coca-Cola out of any other country in the world.

461. Bees kill people more than snakes do.

462. A giraffe does not have any vocal cords, so it technically does not have a voice.

463. The longest word that you can type using only your right hand on a keyboard is "lollipop."

464. The only way you are able to see a rainbow is if your back is facing the sun.

465. The people who work at night are more likely to weigh more than those who work during the day.

466. We use up to 72 different muscles when we speak.

467. The Mona Lisa took Leonardo Da Vinci precisely ten years to paint.

468. There are over 50 million monkeys in India.

469. Giraffes tend to have the highest blood pressure out of any other animal.

470. A shark can smell a single drop of blood in the water from up to 2.5 miles away.

471.

472. A bottlenose whale is capable of diving to around 3,000 feet under the water in about two minutes.

473. You can tell the difference between a female and a male horse by looking at their teeth. A female has 36 teeth while a male has 40.

474. When two zebras are standing together, they will face each other so they can keep an eye out for predators.

475. Elephants communicate in a sound wave that is below the frequency that humans can hear, so we cannot hear them talking to each other.

476. A snake cannot bite you if it is in a river or a swamp; it will drown if it tries.

477. A flea is able to accelerate up to 50 times faster than a space shuttle can.

478. The colder the room you sleep in, the higher your chances are for having a nightmare.

479. Both sides of your body are not usually the same size. Your left side will sometimes be bigger than your right side. In other words, your left foot, or your left hand, will be slightly larger than your right one.

480. In the country of Sweden, high school students get paid around $187 a month just to actually go to school.

481. Billboards have been banned in the state of Vermont for over 45 years in order to preserve the state's natural beauty.

482. NASA has its own radio station that is called the "Third Rock Radio."

483. Carrots were first grown in ancient Greece to use as medicine, not to be eaten.

484. When Coca-Cola was originally released in 1886, it was advertised as an "intellectual beverage" which was supposed to help boost brain power.

485. Over a third of the world's pineapples come from Hawaii.

486. Coca-Cola would actually be green if they did not add the colorant.

487. The guy who invented the cereal Corn Flakes was named John Kellogg.

488. The color of a chili pepper has nothing to do with how hot it is; the size does. Usually the smaller the pepper, the hotter it is.

489. The ideal temperature that will help you fall asleep is between 64 and 86 degrees Fahrenheit.

490. Honey will enter your bloodstream only 20 minutes after you have eaten it.

491. Each one of your red blood cells travels between the lungs and other tissues around 75,000 times before it dies. They only live about four months each.

492. Enamel is the hardest substance in the human body.

493. The earth is hit by over 500 meteorites every year.

494. Clouds are higher in the sky during the day than they are at night.

495. Human blood is about six times thicker than water is.

496. Mercury is the only metal that can become liquid when at room temperature.

497. A "plenum" is the opposite of a "vacuum."

498. The average person will swallow around 295 times while eating a meal.

499. Potato chips are the most popular snack food in the entire world.

500. About 72% of people in the world will eavesdrop on someone.

CONFUSING FACTS FOR GENIUSES

502. An African grey parrot's vocabulary contains just over 200 words.

503. Fire is able to move faster going uphill than going downhill.

504. A crocodile, like most other lizards, only grows as large as its environment allows it to. If it is placed in a small enclosure it will never outgrow that enclosure.

505. There are more deaths caused by hippopotamuses than any other animal in Africa.

506. The human brain contains an average of 78% water.

507. There are more births in August than in any other month.

508. Unless food mixes with your saliva, you will not be able to taste it.

509. Up to 8% of people on Earth are born with an extra rib.

510. Hawaiians only have 13 letters in their alphabet.

511. Armadillos always give birth to only four babies at a time.

512. "Dreamt" is the only word in the entire English language that ends with the letters "mt."

513. Goldfish are capable of seeing both ultraviolet light and infrared light.

514. The human body's smallest bones are found in the ear.

515. "Stewardesses" is the longest word that can be typed using only the left hand.

516. The original name for the internet was ARPANet, which stands for Advanced Research Projects Agency Network.

517. The internet was originally designed for use by the U.S. Department of Defense.

518. One nautical knot out on the ocean is the same as 1.150 miles on land.

519. "The quick brown fox jumps over the lazy dog" is a sentence that uses all of the letters of the alphabet.

520. There are as many as 26 bones in your foot. That is one-fourth of your body's bones.

521. If you add up all of the numbers from one to 100, together it equals 5,050.

522. Your tongue heals faster than any other part of your body.

523. The number "one googol" is basically one followed by 100 zeros.

524. The largest organ on the human body is the skin.

525. People throw coins into the Trevi Fountain found in Italy, and the coins are collected for charity.

526. Every day is considered a holiday somewhere in the world.

527. "Laser" is not just a word; it actually stands for Light Amplification by Stimulated Emission of Radiation.

528. The bone in your throat, known as the hyoid bone, is the only bone in your body that is not attached to another bone.

529. The word "town" is the oldest word in the English language.

530. There are only four words in the English language that end with the letters "d," "o," "u," and "s"; horrendous, tremendous, hazardous, and stupendous.

531. The most sensitive finger on your hand is your index finger.

532. The words "listen" and "silent" both use the same letters.

533. The first boats that were built for sailing were built in Egypt.

534. You can fill a matchbox with gold and then use the same amount of gold to thinly cover a tennis court.

535. White cats born with blue eyes are usually also born deaf.

536. A human body that weighs approximately 154 pounds will contain about 0.2 milligrams of gold.

537. A dentist invented the electric chair.

538. The past tense of the word "dare" is the word "durst."

539. Wind will not make a sound until it blows against something.

540. Humans started naming hurricanes and tropical storms around the year 1953.

541. Almond is a member of the same family as a peach.

542. Gold is known as the only heavy element that will never erode.

543. When you freeze water, it expands by 9% of its original volume.

544. The only vitamin that an egg does not contain is vitamin C.

545. You have to climb 1,792 steps to reach the top of the Eiffel Tower.

546. There are 2,500,000 rivets holding the Eiffel Tower together.

547. It takes 50 years for an oak tree to start producing acorns.

548. The word "almost" is the longest English word that is spelled with the letters in alphabetical order.

549. If human DNA was stretched out into a single line, it would be able to reach the moon 6,000 times.

550. Your tongue is like your fingerprints; it is unique to you.

551. If your body loses 1% of water, you will start to feel thirsty.

552. A dolphin can reach speeds of up to 37 miles per hour.

553. About 10% of your taste buds live on your cheeks.

554. New Zealand has about 70 million sheep and only four million people.

555. Wine spoils when it is exposed to light, which is why wine is sold in tinted bottles.

556. Sound is able to travel through water 4.3 times faster than it can travel through the air.

557. 600,000 to one are the odds of you being struck by lightning.

558. The most active muscles in your body are the muscles that are in your eyes.

559. You can find vitamin B12 in the rain.

560. Your brain requires at least 25% of the oxygen that you breathe.

561. Your liver is used for over 500 different functions.

562. A horse has 18 more bones in its body than humans do.

563. Hydrogen atoms are so small that you need two million of them to fully cover a full stop.

564. The first book printed in England was about chess.

565. The average human body has 59,650 miles of blood vessels.

566. Your stomach acid is strong enough to dissolve a whole nail.

567. When you are typing on a keyboard, 56% of the typing is done with your left hand.

568. There are over six million dust mites in the average bed.

569. 27% of food is thrown away in developed countries.

570. The reason ice skating rinks will always go counter-clockwise is so that right-handed people, who make up the majority, can grab hold of the railing with their right hand.

571. A chameleon uses its tongue to eat, and its tongue is up to twice the length of its body.

572. When you recognize a person's face, you are using the right side of your brain to do so.

573. You cannot read in your dreams because reading and dreaming actually use two different parts of your brain.

574. A caterpillar has more muscles than a human does.

575. Every one square inch of your skin contains up to 625 sweat glands.

576. Your body temperature should normally be 99 degrees Fahrenheit.

577. Gasoline and coffee are the two items that are bought and sold the most throughout the world.

578. In order to make the sound of a cracking whip, the tip of the whip must be traveling faster than the speed of sound.

579. The machine that is used to measure blood is called a "sphygmomanometer."

580. Minus 40 degrees Fahrenheit is exactly the same temperature as minus 40 degrees Celsius.

581. We only started using ignition keys to start cars in the year 1949.

582. A jumbo jet contains enough gasoline in a full tank for a car to drive around the whole world about four times.

583. When Isaac Newton first discovered the law of gravity, he was only 23 years old.

584. 90% of the human body is made up of oxygen, hydrogen, carbon, and nitrogen.

585. The first lie detector was invented in the year 1921.

586. Red light has a higher wavelength than any other light.

587. If a car is traveling about 50 miles per hour, it will use half of its fuel just to overcome the wind resistance.

588. Light is just electromagnetic radiation.

589. Most cats can retract their claws; a cheetah is the only cat that cannot.

590. We are not sure, but it is likely that scissors were invented in ancient Egypt.

591. It's not the air that causes super glue to dry; it's moisture.

592. 7,000 tons of old and worn out currency is shredded in the United States each year.

593. One ton of cement is poured for every woman, man, and child in the world each year.

594. The average human will consume at least 12,000 gallons of water and 100 tons of food in their lifetime.

595. All letters have one syllable except for the letter "W" which has three syllables.

596. One letter out of every eight letters used when writing or typing is an "E."

597. Most of the vitamin C in fruit can be found in the skin.

598. The words "bump" and "assassination" were invented by Shakespeare.

599. When a baby is born, it has 350 bones. By the time a child turns five years old, some bones have merged together, giving the child only 206 bones, which is the normal amount for an adult human.

600. There is a phenomenon called "ghost apples," in which water freezes around an apple during the colder months, and the apple rots away inside the frozen water. This leaves an apple-shaped ghost-like form of ice.

601. The value of the number "pi" was known to only 35 decimal places during the 17th century. Today, it is known to 1.2411 trillion decimal places.

FACTS ABOUT WORLD CITIES

603. There are 456 cities with populations of 1 million or more.

604. Tokyo was once a small fishing village. Today, it has the most populated metropolitan area in the world at more than 37 million people.

605. The city of Shanghai is the most populous city, with more than 24 million people.

606. El Alto, Bolivia, is the highest city in the world. It is 13,615 feet (4,150 meters) above sea level.

607. Bolivia also has the world's highest capital city. La Paz is 11,942 feet (3,640 meters) above sea level.

608. Jericho, in Palestine, is the lowest city in the world. It lies 846 feet (258 meters) below sea level.

609. Baku, Azerbaijan, is the lowest capital city in the world. It lies 92 feet (28 meters) below sea level.

610. Baku is also the largest city in the world located below sea level.

611. Urumqi, China, is the farthest city from the sea. It is 1,600 miles (2,500 km) from the coast.

612. Norilsk, Russia, is the most northern city in the world.

613. Reykjavik, Iceland, is the northernmost capital city.

614. Ushuaia, Argentina, is the southernmost city in the world.

615.

616. Punta Arenas, Chile, is the southernmost large city.

617. The southernmost capital city is Wellington, New Zealand.

618. The unofficial slogan of Austin, Texas, is "Keep Austin Weird."

619. New York has the largest population of any city in the United States, at almost 9 million people in 2019.

620. Los Angeles is a distant second with just over four million.

621. Chicago, Houston, Phoenix, Philadelphia, San Antonio, San Diego, Dallas, and San Jose round out the top ten.

622. The northernmost city in the United States is Bellingham, Washington.

623. The southernmost city in the United States is Key West, Florida.

624. Bangkok, Thailand's full name is the longest city name in the world. Its full name is Krung Thep Mahanakhon Amon Rattanakosin Mahinthara Ayuthaya Mahadilok Phop Noppharat Ratchathani Burirom Udomratchaniwet Mahasathan Amon Piman Awatan Sathit Sakkathattiya Witsanukam Prasit.

625. New York has the largest street network in the world. It measures more than 6200 miles (10,000 km).

626. Los Angeles's full name is El Pueblo de Nuestra Senora la Reina de los Angeles de Porciuncula.

627. There are no cemeteries in San Francisco. The city banned burials in 1900 because it was running out of room. More than 150,000 bodies were relocated to the little town of Colma.

628. Vatican City is the smallest city in the world. It covers only 0.17 square mile (0.44 square km).

629. The capital city with the lowest population is Adamstown in the Pitcairn Islands. Only 48 people live there.

630. Hum, Croatia, has the lowest population of any city. Fewer than 30 people live there.

631. London has the oldest subway system in the world. Its Underground opened in 1863.

632. Boston has the oldest subway in the United States. It opened in 1897.

633. Sao Paolo, Brazil, is the largest city in South America.

634. The oldest city in North America is Cholula, Mexico. It was founded in the second century BC, more than 2,000 years ago.

635. The oldest US city founded by Europeans is St. Augustine, Florida. It was settled by the Spanish in 1565.

636. Juneau, Alaska, is the largest state capital in terms of area. It covers 3,255 square miles (8,430 square km). That's larger than the state of Delaware!

637. Sitka, Alaska, is the largest city in the United States in terms of area.

638. Phoenix, Arizona, used to be called Pumpkinville.

639. Little Rock, Arkansas, has the largest pedestrian bridge in North America.

640. Honolulu, Hawaii, is home to the only royal palace in the United States.

641. Many British colonial cities in America were named after cities in England or after English kings and queens.

642. The first drive-through in America opened in Springfield, Illinois, in 1921.

643. Des Moines, Iowa, was almost named Fort Raccoon.

644. Every summer, Annapolis, Maryland, hosts the largest crab feast in the world.

645. America's oldest wooden fort, Old Fort Western, was built in Augusta, Maine, in 1754.

646. Saint Paul, Minnesota, was called Pig's Eye Landing during the 1800s.

647. Santa Fe, New Mexico, is home to the oldest church in America. Mission San Miguel was built in the 1600s.

648. Salem, Oregon, has one of the smallest parks in the world. Waldo Park measures 12 feet by 20 feet (4 by 6 meters) and has just one tree.

649. Yakutsk, Russia, is the coldest city. The lowest temperature recorded there was −88°F (−64°C).

650. Ulaanbaatar, Mongolia, is the coldest capital city.

651. Ahvaz, Iran, and Kuwait City, Kuwait, are the two hottest cities in the world. Both cities often have temperatures above 113°F (45°C) and often hit 122°F (50°C).

652. In 2014, Kuwait City had a high temperature of more than 125°F (52°C).

653. Minneapolis is considered the most literate city in the United States.

654. Cincinnati, Ohio, was the first city to provide ambulance service in 1865.

655. The first gas station opened in Pittsburgh in 1913.

656. opened in 1909.

657. Here's another first for Pittsburgh—the first commercial radio station started broadcasting there in 1920.

658. The first electric company opened in New York City in 1878.

659. The nation's first hospital opened in Philadelphia in 1752.

660. Philadelphia also boasts the nation's first daily newspaper, which began in 1784.

661. Boston had the first lighthouse in the United States. It opened in 1716.

662. The first movie theater opened in Los Angeles in 1902.

663.

664. The Ferris Wheel made its first appearance at the Chicago World's Fair in 1893.

665. Chicago is also home to the first skyscraper, which opened in 1885.

666. If you wanted to watch public television in 1953, you had to go to Houston, Texas. It was the first city with a noncommercial TV station.

667. The first traffic light was located in Cleveland, Ohio, in 1914.

668. America's first zoo opened in Philadelphia in 1874. It is still operating today.

669. In 2017, El Paso, Texas, was ranked the safest big city in the United States.

670. What city was ranked the most dangerous? Detroit, Michigan.

671. Asia is home to seven of the top ten most populated cities. They are: Shanghai, Beijing, Istanbul, Karachi, Mumbai, Guangzhou, and Delhi.

672. Shanghai, China, is the world's busiest trading port.

673. Tokyo has the world's busiest train station.

674. Tokyo (including suburbs) has the most populous metropolitan area in the world.

675. Seoul, South Korea, has the second-most-populous metro area (including suburbs).

676. Paris is the most popular tourist city in Europe.

677. More than 300 languages are spoken in London.

678. The world has 33 megacities. These are cities with populations of more than 10 million.

679. In 2016, Vienna, Austria, was named the city with the best quality of life.

680. The next-largest South American city is Lima, Peru.

681. People ride boats in the canals for public transit in Venice.

682. All of Australia's major cities lie on or near the coast.

683. Sydney is the largest city in Australia.

684. Sydney is also the oldest Australian city. It was founded in 1788.

685. Perth, Australia, has the largest city park in the world. It covers 10,003 acres (4 square km).

686. Melbourne and Sydney both wanted to be the capital of Australia. In the end, a new capital city, Canberra, was built.

687. Canberra was named Australia's capital in 1913. But the government didn't move there until 1927.

688. Most of Australia's major cities were settled by convicts shipped there from Great Britain.

689. Lagos, Nigeria, is the largest city in Africa. More than 21 million people live there.

690. The second-largest city in Africa is Cairo, Egypt.

691. Cape Town, South Africa, is the southernmost city in Africa.

692. Moscow, Russia, has more billionaires than any other city in the world.

693. The busiest subway systems in the world are in Tokyo, Seoul, and Moscow.

694. More than 6 million people ride Moscow's metro (subway) every day.

695. St. Petersburg, Russia, has more than 1,000 bridges.

696. St. Petersburg is the northernmost city with more than 1 million people.

697. Russia has at least 15 "secret" cities that do not appear on any maps.

698. St. Petersburg has had three different names. Its name was changed to Petrograd in 1914. That name honored Russian czar Peter the Great.

699. In 1924, Petrograd became Leningrad to honor Communist leader Vladimir Ilyich Lenin.

700. Finally, in 1991, the city's name was changed back to St. Petersburg.

701. St. Petersburg isn't the only name-changing Russian city. Stalingrad was named after the Russian leader Joseph Stalin. It was the site of a major World War II battle.

702. In 1961, Stalingrad's name was changed to Volgograd, after the Volga River. Stalin was a cruel dictator, and the government wanted to erase his name from the country.

703. In 2013, Russia agreed to call the city "Stalingrad" for a few days in honor of the seventieth anniversary of the Battle of Stalingrad.

704. Even though they are very crowded, many cities have been called lonely places to live.

FANTASTIC FOOD FACTS

706. Ketchup was once used as medicine.

707. Crackers have holes in them so air bubbles don't break the crackers while they are baking.

708. White chocolate is not really chocolate. It contains no cacao beans.

709. Bananas are classified as berries.

710. Strawberries, raspberries, and blackberries technically aren't berries.

711. American cheese was actually invented in Switzerland.

712. The Aztecs used cocoa beans as money.

713. The fear of getting peanut butter stuck to the roof of your mouth is called arachibutyrophobia.

714. Americans eat millions of pounds of peanut butter every year.

715. Three Musketeers bars originally had three flavors: vanilla, chocolate, and strawberry.

716. Froot Loops are all the same flavor.

717. Ancient Egyptians paid workers with radishes, onions, and garlic.

718. Pasta comes in 350 different shapes.

719. Margherita pizza is named after Queen Margherita of Italy.

720. Margherita pizza includes the colors of the Italian flag: red (sauce), white (cheese), and green (basil).

721. To test eggs, place them in a glass of cold water. Bad eggs will float, but fresh eggs will sink.

722. Ripe cranberries bounce.

723. Human DNA is 60 percent the same as a banana's.

724. Goat meat is the most popular meat in the world.

725. Food is legally allowed to contain a small portion of insects.

726. Australians eat the most meat of any nation.

727. Indians eat the least amount of meat.

728. One hamburger can contain meat from many different cows.

729. The red dye in Skittles is made from boiled beetles.

730. Pound cake got its name because the original recipe called for one pound each of butter, sugar, and eggs.

731. Cheese is the most stolen food. About 4 percent of cheese in the world ends up being stolen.

732. An ear of corn has an even number of rows, usually 16.

733. An 11-year-old boy invented the Popsicle in 1905. He accidentally left a mixture of soda and water outside overnight, and it froze.

734. Potatoes absorb and reflect wireless signals the same way humans do.

735. Honey never goes bad.

736. In the eighteenth century, Europeans called tomatoes "the poison apple" and were afraid to eat them.

737. Grapes will explode in the microwave.

738. The earliest reference to soup comes from 6,000 BC. It included hippo and sparrow meat.

739. Apples belong to the rose family.

740. So do pears and plums.

741. A cheese called Casu Marzu contains maggots.

742. The twists in pretzels are made to look like arms crossed in prayer.

743. Apples are 25 percent air.

744. Worldwide, there are over 7,500 different varieties of apple.

745. There are more than 3,000 varieties of pear.

746. Cucumbers are 96 percent water.

747. Spam is short for "spiced ham."

748. Tuna eyeballs are a popular snack in Japan.

749. Dry swallowing sugar can cure hiccups.

750. Almonds are not nuts. They are seeds.

751. Peanuts aren't nuts either. They're legumes.

752. Peanuts contain an oil that is used to make dynamite.

753. An American named Thomas Sullivan created the tea bag. He sent small bags of tea to customers as samples.

754. Many food companies use flavorists, scientists whose job is to use chemistry to create and improve food.

755. If you eat way too many carrots, your skin can turn orange.

756. Potatoes were the first vegetables planted in space.

757. Carrots were originally purple.

758. Lollipops have been around for thousands of years.

759. Thomas Jefferson introduced macaroni and cheese to America. He originally had the dish in France.

760. Lobsters were once so common that they were considered a cheap food for the poor and for prisoners.

761. Raw lima beans are poisonous.

762. McDonald's sells 2.5 billion hamburgers a year.

763. That works out to 6.5 million hamburgers a day, or 75 hamburgers every second.

764. Pistachios aren't nuts. They are the seeds of a fruit.

765. Caesar salad was created in Mexico and gets its name from its creator, Caesar Cardini.

766. Americans eat about 20 million hot dogs a year.

767. Ice cream cones were invented at the 1904 World's Fair, when an ice cream vendor ran out of bowls and asked a waffle vendor for help.

768. Astronaut John Young smuggled a corned beef sandwich into space. But when he tried to eat it, the sandwich fell apart because there was no gravity to hold it together.

769. Lemons float because they have the same density as water.

770. Popcorn was the first food to be microwaved.

771. Garlic is a natural insect repellent.

772. Broccoli contains more protein than steak.

773. A tube of applesauce was the first food eaten in space.

774. The first meal eaten on the moon included a peach, bacon squares, sugar cookie cubes, coffee, and pineapple-grapefruit drinks.

HOT AND COLD FACTS

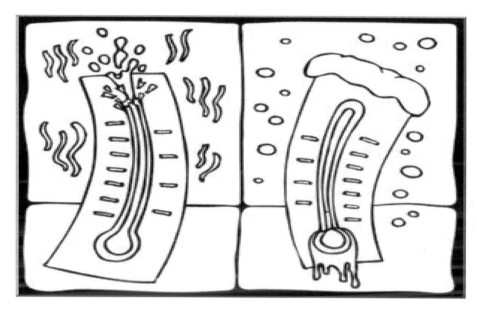

776.Heat happens when energy is burned or used.

777.The hotter an object, the faster its molecules are moving.

778.Heat makes objects expand. Cold makes them contract.

779.Conduction occurs when heat transfers from one object to another until they are the same temperature.

780.Pots and pans are made from metal because metal conducts heat very well.

781.Heat and cold can change states of matter. Objects can melt if they get too hot. They freeze if they get very cold.

782.There are three different temperature scales: Fahrenheit, Celsius, and Kelvin.

783.On the Fahrenheit scale, water freezes at 32°and boils at 212°.

784.On the Celsius scale, water freezes at 0° and boils at 100°.

785. The Kelvin scale is used mostly by scientists because it does not include negative numbers.

786. Water freezes at 273.15°K.

787. It boils at 373.15°K.

788. 0°K is known as absolute zero. At that temperature, all motion stops.

789. The hottest temperature ever recorded on Earth was 134°F (57°C) in Death Valley, California, in 1913.

790. Energy from lightning heats the air up to 60,000°F (33,316°C).

791. Venus is the hottest planet in the solar system.

792. Its surface temperature is a toasty 854°F (457°C).

793. Mercury is the closest planet to the Sun, but it has a thinner atmosphere than Venus. That means the planet doesn't hold in as much heat.

794. Still, Mercury's temperature can rise as high as 801°F (427°C).

795. The temperature at the core of the Sun can be as hot as 27 million °F (15 million °C).

796. The temperature of the surface of the sun is about 10,000°F (5,600°C).

797. The bright light that can be seen during a solar eclipse is called the corona. Its temperature measures between two and 17 million °F (2 to 10 million °C).

798. Scientists think the highest possible temperature is 142 nonillion Kelvins.

799. That's 142 followed by 30 zeroes.

800. The Sahara is the world's largest hot desert.

801. The Ring of Fire is an area in the Pacific Ocean. Three-quarters of the Earth's active volcanoes are found there.

802. A magnifying glass can concentrate the sun's rays enough to start a fire.

803. The hottest sea in the world is the Red Sea. Its warmest spot is 87°F (31°C).

804. A heat wave occurs when temperatures are 9°F (5°C) above average for at least five days in a row.

805. The first use of the term heat wave was in New York City in 1892.

806. The world's hottest pepper is the infinity chili.

807. Fire tornadoes happen when super-hot heat and high winds spin air and debris into a whirling column.

808. Firefighters go into super-hot places. Their protective gear can weigh up to 60 pounds (27 kg).

809. Gold melts at about 1,947°F (1,064°C).

810. Pure silver melts at 1,761°F (961°C).

811. Tungsten is the hardest metal to melt. It has to reach 6,150°F (3,400°C) to melt.

812. Hot coals can reach temperatures of about 1,000°F (537°C).

813. People who walk on hot coals rarely get burned because most of the heat doesn't transfer to their feet.

814. More than half of the homes in the United States are heated by natural gas.

815. Other sources of heat include electricity, propane, oil, and wood.

816. The Chinese were the first to use natural gas for heat, around 500 BC. They built pipes to transport gas coming out of the ground into their homes.

817. During the last Ice Age, one-third of the Earth's surface was covered in ice.

818. Today, ice only covers about one-tenth of the Earth's surface.

819. Water boils at just 10 degrees above freezing on Mars.

820. Early hockey pucks were made of frozen cow poop.

821. Some frogs have special antifreeze-like chemicals in their blood. This allows them to freeze almost solid during the winter.

822. A New Zealand insect called the weta freezes solid in the winter and thaws out when the weather warms up.

823. Brain freeze occurs when something really cold touches a nerve in the roof of your mouth.

824. The lowest temperature ever recorded on Earth was −128.6°F (−89.2°C) in Antarctica.

825. Almost all of the world's glacial ice is found in Greenland and Antarctica.

826. Even though they're found in the ocean, icebergs are mostly made of fresh water.

827. In some parts of Antarctica, the ice is 3 miles (5 km) thick.

828. The 30-30-30 rule says that if the temperature is −30°F (−34.4°C) and the wind is blowing at 30 miles (48.3 km) per hour, human skin freezes in 30 seconds.

829. Some animals' fur changes to white during the winter to help them hide in the snow.

830. Some of these animals include the arctic fox, arctic hare, ptarmigan, and ermine.

831. Icebergs are bigger than 16 feet (5 meters) across. Bergy bits are less than 16 feet (5 meters). Growlers are chunks of ice less than 6.6 feet (2 meters) wide.

832. The largest snowflake ever recorded measured 15 inches (38 cm) wide and 8 inches (20 cm) thick. It fell in 1887 in Montana.

833. Snowflakes fall at a speed of about 3 miles (5 km) per hour.

834. One inch (2.54 cm) of snow melts down to just 1/10-inch (0.254 cm) of water.

835. A single snowstorm can drop 39 million tons of snow.

836. Snow is actually ice crystals stuck together.

837. Snow looks white because of light bouncing off the ice crystals.

838. All snowflakes have six sides.

839. The record for the most snow in the United States in a 24-hour period is 76 inches (193 cm) in Silver Lake, Colorado. The big storm occurred in 1921.

840. Mount Baker Ski Area in Washington state received 1,140 inches (2,896 cm) of snow during the 1998–1999 season. That's a world record!

841. Antarctica is the coldest continent.

842. Russia is the coldest country.

843. The next four coldest countries are Canada, Mongolia, Finland, and Iceland.

844. A hotel in Sweden is made from a mix of snow and ice. Everything inside is also made of ice.

845. The hotel melts every spring and is rebuilt every winter.

846. The coldest temperature recorded in the United States was –80°F (–62°C) near Fairbanks, Alaska, in 1971.

847. The coldest US temperature outside of Alaska occurred in Rogers Pass, Montana, in 1954. It was a bone-chilling –70°F (–57°C).

848. Hawaii is the only state to never see a temperature below zero.

849. The coldest temperature ever recorded in Hawaii was 12°F (−11°C) at the Mauna Kea Observatory on May 17, 1979.

850. The coldest temperature in North America occurred in the Yukon territory of Canada on February 3, 1947, when the thermometer plunged to −81.4°F (−63°C)

SUPER SOCCER FACTS

852. The earliest versions of soccer can be traced back 3,000 years.

853. The British established the rules for modern soccer in 1863.

854. In most parts of the world, soccer is called football.

855. Soccer is the most popular game in the world.

856. More than 250 million people in 200 countries play soccer.

857. At any point during a soccer game, 11 players should be on the field for each team.

858. Only the goalie can touch the ball with their hands.

859. Other players use their feet, bodies, and heads to move the ball.

860. Soccer is the only major sport where players can't use their hands to move the ball.

861. In Europe during the Middle Ages, soccer balls were made from inflated pig bladders.

862. In ancient China, soccer balls were made of clothes filled with rubble.

863. A traditional soccer ball has 32 panels.

864. Each panel represents a nation in Europe.

865. Soccer balls are actually slightly oval in shape. The pattern on the ball makes it look round.

866. An international soccer game is 90 minutes long.

867. The game is divided into two 45-minute halves.

868. A regulation soccer field must be between 100 to 130 yards (91 to 119 meters) long and 50 to 100 yards (46 to 91 meters) wide.

869. The Fédération Internationale de Football Association (FIFA) governs international soccer.

870. FIFA sponsors the World Cup championships.

871. The World Cup is the most-watched sporting event in the world.

872. The first World Cup was held in Uruguay in 1930. Uruguay won.

873. Brazilian star Pelé is considered to be the best soccer player of all time.

874. Pelé played in his first World Cup in 1958 when he was 17. He was the youngest to ever play in a World Cup game.

875. He scored six goals and led Brazil to victory.

876. After the 1958 World Cup, Brazil declared Pelé a national treasure to prevent him from playing for any other country.

877. Pelé scored 1,280 goals in 1,360 games during his career.

878. The Women's World Cup was created in 1991.

879. The United States has won more Women's World Cups than any other country.

880. The 1999 Women's World Cup final was the most-watched soccer game in US television history.

881. Soccer matches in England did not have referees until 1881. Instead, they relied on good sportsmanship.

882. FIFA uses a microchip in the ball and sensors in the goal to track the ball to make sure a goal is actually scored.

883. As of 2018, the World Cup has only been held outside of South America or Europe three times in its history.

884. Those three events were held in the United States, South Africa, and jointly between Japan and South Korea.

885. Only seven countries have won the men's World Cup.

886. Those countries are Uruguay, Italy, Brazil, Germany, Argentina, England, and Spain.

887. Approximately 1.1 billion people watched the 2006 World Cup final.

888. More than 3 million young people play soccer in the United States.

889. The biggest blowout in soccer history was a 149-0 score between two teams in Madagascar.

890. Soccer players can run up to 9.5 miles (15 km) in a single match.

891. The first soccer goals were wicker baskets

WILD AND WEIRD WEATHER FACTS

893. All weather is caused by heat from the sun and movement of the air.

894. Weather happens in the lowest level of the Earth's atmosphere.

895. As the sun warms the air, that warm air rises.

896. Cold air rushes in underneath the warm air.

897. This movement creates wind.

898. Water evaporates on Earth and then rises as water vapor to form clouds.

899. There are six main components of weather.

900. They are temperature, atmospheric pressure, wind, humidity, precipitation, and cloudiness.

901. Scientists who study the weather are called meteorologists.

902. The coldest weather is usually found at the North and South Poles.

903. The warmest weather is usually found at the Equator.

904. A high-pressure weather system usually brings clear skies.

905. A low-pressure system usually brings storms.

906. Wind tends to blow from areas of high pressure to areas of low pressure.

907. Strong winds called the jet stream occur in the upper atmosphere, about 5 to 9 miles (8 to 15 km) above the Earth.

908. These winds push weather systems around the Earth.

909. Jet-stream winds usually blow at 80 to 140 miles (129 to 225 km) per hour.

910. Jet-stream winds can reach top speeds of more than 275 miles (443 km) per hour.

911. Because of the jet stream, weather systems usually move from east to west.

912. However, weather systems can move in any direction.

913. Humidity is the amount of moisture in the air.

914. When there is 100 percent humidity, it will rain. That's because the atmosphere cannot hold any more water.

915. Clouds come in a variety of forms. Not all of them produce precipitation.

916. Cirrus clouds are thin, wispy clouds. They usually signal mild weather.

917. Nimbostratus clouds produce steady precipitation over a period of time.

918. Enormous cumulonimbus clouds, or thunderheads, release heavy downpours.

919. Cumulonimbus clouds can also produce thunderstorms and tornadoes.

920. Because clouds affect the amount of sunlight reaching the Earth's surface, cloudy days are cooler than clear ones.

921. The opposite is true at night, when clouds act as a blanket, keeping the Earth warm.

922. Heat waves can bend train tracks.

923. Heat waves can also ground planes.

924. Hot air is less dense than cold air, so planes can have trouble taking off and landing in extreme heat.

925. You can figure out the temperature by counting a cricket's chirps and using a number of different formulas.

926. Sandstorms can swallow up entire cities.

927. A 2003 heat wave turned grapes into raisins.

928. Lightning often occurs after a volcanic eruption.

929. It sometimes rains frogs or fish.

930. This happens when a waterspout picks up animals from one place and drops them in another.

931. In July 2001, a blood-red rain fell in India.

932. The red color might have been caused by bits from a meteorite, or sand from the desert.

933. In 2015, a milky rain fell on parts of Washington, Oregon, and Idaho. The strange rain was caused by chemicals in a dust storm.

934. In England in 1894, jellyfish rained from the sky.

935. Eight alligators fell from the sky over South Carolina in 1887.

936. Rain contains vitamin B12.

937. Windstorms include tornadoes, dust devils, squalls, and gales.

938. Storms with a lot of precipitation include hailstorms, ice storms, snowstorms, blizzards, ocean storms, thunderstorms, and hurricanes.

939. Christopher Columbus encountered a tropical cyclone in 1494.

940. Columbus's notes were the first written account of this type of storm by a European.

941. Robert Fitzroy was the first weather forecaster.

942. Fitzroy was appointed to the position in England in 1860.

943. Fitzroy also started the practice of printing the weather forecast in daily newspapers.

944. In some mountains in Colorado and California, algae mixes with snow and turns it pink.

945. Sometimes lightning forms a ball. Scientists don't know what causes ball lightning.

946. Ball lightning was first captured on film in 2012.

947. Arica, Chile, went for 14 years without any rain.

948. Wind doesn't make a sound unless it blows against an object.

949. Fire whirls are tornadoes caused by wildfires.

950. It was so cold in 1684 that the Thames River in England froze solid for two months.

951. In 1932, it was so cold that Niagara Falls froze solid.

952. A cubic mile (4 cubic km) of fog contains less than a gallon of water.

953. In 1899, the Mississippi River froze down its entire length.

954. Chunks of ice were seen in the Gulf of Mexico.

955. The 1899 cold spell has been called the greatest cold snap in American history.

956. Snowflakes can take up to an hour to reach the ground.

957. The windiest city in the United States is Mt. Washington, New Hampshire, with an average wind speed of 35 miles (56 km) per hour.

958. The least windy city is Oak Ridge, Tennessee, with an average wind speed of 4 miles (6 km) per hour.

959. Weather balloons have been used to observe the atmosphere since the late 1930s.

960. Weather balloons are also called radiosondes.

961. Radiosondes are released two times a day from about a thousand locations around the world.

962. The US National Weather Service sends up radiosondes from more than 90 weather stations across the country.

963. In the United States, the Citizen Weather Observer Program depends on amateur meteorologists with homemade weather stations and Internet connections to provide forecasts.

964. The first weather satellite was launched on April 1, 1960.

965. Geostationary satellites track the weather over one region.

966. Other satellites orbit the Earth every 12 hours. They trace weather patterns over the entire part of the globe they orbit.

967. Conventional radar shows clouds and precipitation.

968. Doppler radar measures changes in wind speed and direction.

969. Doppler radar provides information within a range of about 143 miles (230 km).

970. Doppler radar allows meteorologists to forecast when and where severe thunderstorms and tornadoes develop.

971. Microbursts are powerful winds that originate in thunderstorms.

972. Microbursts are among the most dangerous weather a pilot can encounter.

973. If an aircraft attempts to land or take off through a microburst, the suddenly changing wind conditions can cause the craft to lose lift and crash.

974. In the United States alone, airline crashes because of microbursts have caused more than 600 deaths since 1964.

975. "Red sky in morning, sailors take warning/Red sky at night, sailors delight" is actually a weather prediction.

976. A red sky in the morning shows that the sun is reflecting off rain clouds.

977. A red sky at night indicates clear, calm weather.

978. In 1938, a hurricane formed in the Atlantic Ocean on January 1, making it the earliest-ever hurricane in the calendar year.

979. The heaviest snowfall recorded in Los Angeles occurred on January 10 to 11, 1949.

980. That total snowfall was just 0.3 inch (0.8 cm).

981. The world's biggest snowflake was reportedly observed in Montana in January 1887. A rancher described seeing a 15-inch (38-cm)-wide flake.

982. However, no one knows if the snowflake was actually that big.

983. Scientists used to think no two snowflakes were alike.

984. However, in 1988, a research center identified a set of twin crystals from a Wisconsin storm.

985. The Grand Banks of Newfoundland, Canada, see fog more than 200 days a year.

986. An estimated 1.23 inches (3 cm) of rain fell in a single minute on July 4, 1956, in Unionville, Maryland.

987. In 1925, the "Tri-State Tornado" traveled 219 miles (352 km) from Ellington, Missouri, to Princeton, Indiana, over 3.5 hours.

988. In April 1991, a tornado carried a cancelled personal check for 223 miles (359 km) from Stockton, Kansas, to Winnetoon, Nebraska.

989. A 253-mile (407-km)-per-hour wind gust blew through Barrow Island, Australia, in 1996.

990. Miami, Florida, is the rainiest city in the United States, with an average total of 62 inches (158 cm) per year.

991. The winds that create a tornado form on the ground and work their way up to the clouds.

992. Phoenix, Arizona, receives 211 days of sunshine a year

AWESOME OLYMPICS FACTS

994. Olympic gold medals are mostly made of silver.

995. The Olympic torch relay started in the 1936 Olympics.

996. Only three Olympic Games have been canceled.

997. The Games in 1916, 1940, and 1944 were canceled because of war.

998. The Tokyo 2020 Games were postponed until 2021 because of the COVID-19 virus.

999. Only five nations have competed in every Summer Games.

1000. They are Great Britain, Greece, France, Switzerland, and Australia.

1001. Eddie Eagen is the only person to win gold medals in both Summer and Winter Olympics.

1002. He won a gold in boxing in 1920 and a gold in bobsledding in 1932.

1003. Athletes from the former Soviet Union competed as the Unified Team in the 1992 Summer Games.

1004. Two athletes have won gold medals competing for two different nations.

1005. Daniel Carrol won gold in rugby for Australia in 1908. He won gold again in 1920 for the United States.

1006. Kakhi Kakhiashvili won gold in weightlifting as part of the Unified Team in 1992. He won again as a Greek citizen in 1996 and 2000.

1007. The youngest Olympian was Greek gymnast Dimitrios Loundras. He competed at the 1896 Games when he was just 10 years old.

1008. The youngest to win a gold medal is Marjorie Gestring, who won a diving title at the 1936 Games when she was 13.

1009. Greece won the most medals—47—at the first modern Olympic Games in 1896.

1010. The first Winter Olympics were held in Chamonix, France, in 1924.

1011. Norway has won the most medals at the Winter Games.

1012. The United States has won the most medals at the Summer Games.

1013. From 1924 until 1992, the Summer and Winter Games were held in the same year, every four years. Starting in 1994, the Winter and Summer Games have alternated every two years.

1014. The first Olympics covered by US television was the 1960 Summer Games in Rome, Italy.

1015. No country in the Southern Hemisphere has ever hosted a Winter Olympics.

1016. Australia and Brazil are the only countries in the Southern Hemisphere to host the Olympics.

1017. Africa has never hosted an Olympics.

1018. In the Opening Ceremonies, Greece leads the athletes' procession.

1019. The last team in the procession is the host country's.

1020. Other teams march in alphabetical order in the host country's language.

1021. At the Opening Ceremonies, athletes march in representing their countries. At the Closing Ceremonies, the athletes march in as one big group.

1022. The ancient Olympic Games were held in Greece from 776 BC until 393 AD.

1023. The ancient Games were also a religious festival to honor Zeus.

1024. Events included horse races, wrestling, boxing, foot races, and the pentathlon.

1025. There were no team sports in the ancient Games.

1026. Only free Greek men could compete. No slaves, women, or foreigners.

1027. Ancient Olympic athletes competed naked.

1028. The first modern-day Olympics were held in Greece in 1896.

1029. Baron Pierre de Coubertin founded the modern Olympic Games.

1030. The official languages of the Olympics are English and French.

1031. From 1912 to 1948, artists participated in the Olympics: painters, sculptors, architects, writers, and musicians competed for medals.

1032. The first official Olympic mascot was Waldi, the dachshund, at the 1972 Games in Munich.

1033. The 1896 Olympics saw 245 athletes from 14 countries compete.

1034. All of them were men.

1035. Women joined in at the 1900 Games.

1036. The first women's sports were tennis, sailing, croquet, horseback riding, and golf.

1037. The 2016 Summer Games, held in Brazil, were the first ones held in South America.

1038. Swimmer Michael Phelps has won 16 medals, more than any other athlete.

1039. Fourteen of those medals were gold.

1040. Only men compete in the ten-event decathlon.

1041. Only women compete in the seven-event heptathlon.

1042. Five Olympic athletes have won medals in both the Summer and Winter Games.

1043. All Summer Olympic sports must be popular with men in at least 75 countries on 4 continents and with women in at least 40 countries on 3 continents.

1044. Oscar Swahn is the oldest Olympic medalist. He was 64 when he won gold at a shooting event in 1908.

1045. There are no motorized sports in the Olympics.

1046.   The United States and 65 other nations boycotted the 1980 Olympic Games in Moscow.

1047.   The boycott was caused by the Soviet Union's invasion of Afghanistan.

1048.   The Olympic flag was first flown at the 1920 Games.

1049.   The Olympic motto is "Citius, Altius, Fortius."

1050.   That's Latin for "Swifter, Higher, Stronger."

1051.   At least one of the Olympic Rings' colors appears in every national flag.

1052.   The five Olympic rings represent the Americas, Asia, Europe, Australia, and Africa.

1053.   Tug-of-war was an Olympic event between 1900 and 1920.

1054.   The 1956 Summer Olympics were held in Melbourne, Australia, but all the equestrian events were held in Stockholm, Sweden.

1055.   Strict quarantine rules prevented the horses from entering Australia.

1056.   The 2012 Summer Games were the first where all participating countries sent female athletes.

1057.   All swimming events at the 1896 Games were held in the Bay of Zea.

1058.   Swimmers faced chilly water and big waves.

1059.   A boat took swimmers into the bay, where they jumped into the water.

1060.   The 1900 Olympics featured a swimming obstacle race.

1061.   Other sports that are no longer in the Olympics are club swinging, pistol dueling, live pigeon shooting, rope climbing, and a diving event called the plunge for distance.

1062.   At the 1968 Winter Olympics, three American women tied for second place in the 500-meter speed-skating event. All three stood on the podium and received silver medals.

1063.   In 1960, Abebe Bikila won the marathon while running barefoot. He was the first athlete from Africa to win a gold medal.

MIND-BLOWING FACTS ABOUT THE UNIVERSE

1065.   Space doesn't have a temperature. Only items in space have a temperature.

1066.   Distances in the solar system are calculated using astronomical units, or AUs.

1067.   One AU equals the distance from the Earth to the sun, about 93 million miles (about 150 million km).

1068.   The universe is so big, scientists measure it in light-years.

1069. A light-year is the distance light travels in one year. That's about 5.88 trillion miles (9.46 trillion km).

1070. Venus is the brightest planet in the sky because the thick clouds covering it reflect a lot of sunlight.

1071. Venus has the densest atmosphere of any planet.

1072. The pressure is so great, it could crush you like a soda can.

1073. The three brightest objects in our sky are the sun, the Moon, and Venus.

1074. Our sun is more than four billion years old.

1075. Jupiter, Saturn, Uranus, and Neptune do not have solid surfaces.

1076. These planets are called gas giants.

1077. Their surface is made of gases with just a small, rocky core.

1078. Jupiter has at least fifty moons.

1079. Uranus tilts so much that it looks like it is lying on its side.

1080. Because of its tilt, Uranus has forty-two years of darkness followed by forty-two years of sunshine.

1081. The wind on Neptune blows more than 1,200 miles (2,000 km) per hour.

1082. A supernova is the explosive death of a very large star.

1083. Supernova explosions can cause black holes.

1084. Black holes condense all of a star's matter in a very small space.

1085. The force of gravity in a black hole is so strong that it sucks in everything around it.

1086. Not even light can escape a black hole.

1087. Scientists think there could be up to 100 million black holes in our galaxy alone.

1088. Black holes can grow billions of times bigger than the sun.

1089. The universe is always expanding.

1090. A comet's tail can be hundreds of millions of miles (km) long.

1091. Comets are made of ice, sand, and carbon dioxide.

1092. The Kuiper Belt lies beyond Neptune and has many comets.

1093. The planet Pluto was discovered in 1930.

1094. In 2006, Pluto was demoted to a dwarf planet.

1095. The dwarf planet Eris is the coldest object in our solar system.

1096. Eris orbits the sun once every 557 years.

1097. There are anywhere between 200 and 400 billion stars in the Milky Way.

1098. There are an estimated 100 billion planets in the Milky Way.

1099. Scientists estimate that some planets in the Milky Way could contain liquid water.

1100. That means there could be 8.8 billion planets within the galaxy capable of supporting life.

1101. Since 1991, astronomers have discovered more than 550 planets outside our solar system.

1102. Most galaxies are spiral-shaped.

1103. NASA monitors more than 1,200 potentially hazardous asteroids.

1104. Meteors are space materials that heat up and burn once they enter Earth's atmosphere.

1105. Meteors are also called shooting stars.

1106. Meteorites are meteors that don't burn up completely and make impact on Earth's surface.

1107. The largest meteorite ever found landed in Africa and weighed 119,000 pounds (54,000 kg).

1108. The word planet comes from the Greek planets, which means "wanderer."

1109. A plane ride to Pluto would take more than 800 years.

1110. It's estimated that the universe is 13.7 billion years old.

1111. Only 4 percent of the universe is made up of things we can see, such as stars and planets.

1112. Most of the universe is made of invisible matter, called dark energy and dark matter.

1113. It takes so long for light from some stars to travel to Earth that looking at the night sky is actually a glimpse into the past.

1114. There is no sound in space.

1115. A day on Venus is longer than a year on Venus.

1116. Venus is the only planet that rotates backward.

1117. You could fit 1.3 million Earths inside the sun.

1118. There are more stars in the universe than there are grains of sand on Earth.

1119. Neutron stars are the fastest spinning objects in the universe.

1120. These stars can spin up to six hundred times a second.

1121. A spoonful of matter from a neutron star weighs about a billion tons.

1122. Almost every element found on Earth was created in the burning core of a star.

1123. That means our bodies are made of stardust!

1124. Astronomers estimate that 275 million stars are born and die throughout the observable universe each day.

1125. That adds up to more than 100 billion over the course of a year.

1126. Mercury is super-hot, but it has ice on its surface.

1127. The ice is located in craters that don't receive any sunlight.

1128. Mars's Olympus Mons volcano is the largest in the solar system.

1129. Olympus Mons is 374 miles (602 km) wide. That's the size of Arizona.

1130. The volcano is 16 miles (25 km) high, or triple the height of Mount Everest.

1131. Mars also has the longest valley. Valles Marineris is 2,500 miles (4,000 km) long. That's ten times as long as the Grand Canyon.

1132. Jupiter's Great Red Spot is actually a violent storm.

1133. That storm has been raging for more than three hundred years.

1134. The Great Red Spot is about three times as wide as Earth.

1135. Huge dust storms on Mars can last for months and bury the entire surface.

1136. The winds on Neptune move at more than 1,500 miles (2,414 km) per hour.

1137. Mercury has the most extreme temperature swings of any planet.

1138. The surface of Mercury can reach a scorching 840°F (450°C).

1139. Since Mercury doesn't have enough atmosphere to trap any heat, night-time temperatures can plunge to –275°F (–170°C).

1140. That's more than a 1,100°F (593°C) temperature change.

1141. Pluto is smaller in diameter than the United States.

1142. There are Mars rocks on Earth.

1143. These meteorites might have been blasted from Mars to Earth by a large asteroid strike or a volcanic eruption.

1144. Jupiter has the biggest ocean of any planet.

1145. But it's made of metallic hydrogen.

1146. This ocean is about 25,000 miles (40,000 km) deep.

1147. Mercury is only about as wide as the Atlantic Ocean.

1148. Eighteen Mercurys could fit inside our Earth.

1149. Earth is the only planet not named after a Roman or Greek god or goddess.

1150.   Saturn's rings are made of billions of pieces of ice, dust, and rocks.

1151.   Jupiter, Uranus, and Neptune also have rings, but only Saturn's are visible to us.

1152.   The dwarf planet Haumea, which orbits in the Kuiper Belt, has two moons.

1153.   A day on Haumea only lasts four hours.

1154.   Some astronomers think it's possible for moons to have moons.

1155.   They call these objects moonmoons, moonitos, submoons, grandmoons, moonettes, or moooons.

1156.   Saturn's Hyperion moon gives off static electricity.

1157.   Saturn's moon Pan is disc-shaped because it absorbs some of the particles given off by Saturn's rings.

1158.   In September 2018, astronomers found a long stream of infrared light coming from a neutron star eight hundred light-years away from Earth.

1159.   Ceres is the largest asteroid in our solar system.

1160.   Ceres is 600 miles (966 km) in diameter.

1161.   That's as big as India or Argentina.

1162.   The sun makes up more than 99 percent of our solar system's mass.

1163.   A small asteroid called Chariklo has two icy rings around it.

1164.   All the planets in the solar system could fit between the Earth and the Moon

AMAZING FACTS ABOUT NUMBERS

1166. There is only one even prime number: the number 2.

1167. All other even numbers can be divided by 2.

1168. The largest prime number was discovered in 2018.

1169. The largest prime number is written as M82589933, which is

$$282,589,933 - 1.$$

1170. The word hundred comes from the Old Norse hundrath, but

hundrath actually means "120."

1171. Zero is the only number that can't be represented in Roman

numerals.

1172. That's because ancient cultures did not consider zero to be a

number.

1173. Different cultures discovered zero at different times.

1174. Zero was first used by the Sumerians between 4,000 and 5,000 years ago.

1175. Sumerians didn't use it to represent nothing, though. Instead, they added it to single numbers to denote tens and hundreds.

1176. In the fifth century, an Indian mathematician named Brahmagupta became the first person to use zero as a number.

1177. He represented it with a dot, which he wrote under other numbers.

1178. The number 4 is the only one spelled with the same number of letters as its value.

1179. The number 40 is the only one spelled in alphabetical order.

1180. The number 1 is the only number spelled in reverse alphabetical order.

1181. The number 6 is the smallest perfect number.

1182. That means it is the sum of its integers. 3+2+1=6.

1183. The next perfect number is 28.

1184. An irrational number is a number that can't be written as a fraction.

1185. Pi is an irrational number.

1186. Pi never repeats and never ends.

1187. Leonardo Fibonacci discovered a mathematical sequence that's called the Fibonacci sequence. Starting at 0 and 1, this sequence is created by adding the two preceding numbers in the sequence. 0, 1, 1, 2, 3, 5, 8, 13, 21, 34, etc.

1188.   The Fibonacci sequence appears many times in nature, including flower seeds, pine cones, and animal litters.

1189.   The number 9 is called a "magic number," because when you multiply a number by 9 and add all the digits of the new number together, the sum will always add up to 9.

1190.   The number 7 is the most popular "favorite number."

1191.   Almost 10 percent of people asked picked 7 as their favorite number.

1192.   The number 4 is considered unlucky in Asia because it sounds like the word for "death."

1193.   This equation is interesting! (6x9) + (6+9) = 69.

1194.   And this one is fun! 111,111,111 x 111,111,111 = 12,345,678,987,654,321.

1195.   In a group of 23 people, there's a 50 percent chance that two share the same birthday.

1196.   Most mathematical symbols weren't invented until the sixteenth century.

1197.   Before that, equations were written in words.

1198.   The only number between 0 and 1,000 that has the letter "a" in it is 1,000 (one thousand).

1199.   Every odd number has an "e" in it.

1200.   Markings on animal bones indicate that humans have been doing math since around 30,000 BC.

1201.   The symbol for division (÷) is called an obelus.

1202. A jiffy is an actual unit of time.

1203. A jiffy measures 1/100th of a second.

1204. The numbers 2 and 5 are the only prime numbers that end in 2 or 5.

1205. The number 1 is not a prime number.

1206. If you shuffle a deck of cards properly, the exact order of the cards you get has never been seen before in the whole history of the universe.

1207. A number is an idea.

1208. A numeral is the symbol we use to write a number.

1209. The numerals we use today are based on the Hindu-Arabic system.

1210. That system was developed more than 1,000 years ago.

1211. Different names for zero include nought, naught, zilch, zip, and nil.

1212. A googol is the number one followed by 100 zeroes.

1213. The search engine Google got its name from the number googol.

1214. A googolplex is the number 1 followed by a googol zeroes.

1215. A googolplex is so huge, it can't be written, except by using scientific notation.

1216. The word googol was made up by a nine-year-old in 1920. He came up with the word when his uncle asked him what he could call a 1 followed by 100 zeros.

1217. If you take any number and multiply it by 3, then add up the digits of the new number, the result will always be divisible by 3.

1218. Only 4 colors are needed to color any map.

1219. This fact was discovered in 1853 and was the first major mathematical theorem proved by using a computer in 1976.

1220. Bees can distinguish between 2, 3, and 4 dots.

1221. Leonardo da Vinci used the paint-by-numbers concept to teach his students.

1222. The paint-by-number idea was revived in a series of popular painting kits during the 1940s.

1223. Some cultures have no words for numbers.

1224.   These cultures are called anumeric cultures.

1225.   People with dyscalculia, or "math dyslexia," have trouble understanding numbers.

1226.   The word million was introduced into the English language in the fourteenth century.

1227.   Million comes from the Old French word million and Italian word millione, which means "great thousand."

1228.   The number 5,040 is divisible by 60 numbers.

1229.   The number 5,040 belongs to a rare group of numbers called highly composite numbers or anti-prime numbers.

1230.   The Greek philosopher Plato called 5,040 a "perfect number."

1231.   Prime numbers help an insect called the cicada survive.

1232.   Cicadas incubate underground for long periods of time before coming out to mate. They spend 13 or 17 years underground.

1233.   Both those intervals are prime numbers. Biologists believe cicadas adopted those life cycles to minimize their contact with predators with more round-numbered life cycles.

1234.   Adding up the numbers 1 to 100 gives you the number 5050.

1235.   Pythagoras, the Greek father of math, used little rocks to represent equations.

1236.   The word calculus is the Greek word for "pebbles."

1237.   The word fraction comes from the Latin "fractio," which means "to break."

1238. If you folded a piece of paper in half 103 times, it would be the thickness of the observable universe.

1239. The record for folding a piece of paper in half is just 12 times.

1240. The numbers on opposite sides of a die always add up to 7.

1241. The numbers 1, 2 and 3 all share a vertex on a die.

1242. If these three numbers run clockwise around this vertex, then the die is called left-handed.

1243. If the three numbers run counter-clockwise round the vertex, then it is right-handed.

1244. A three-dimensional parallelogram is called a parallelepiped.

1245. A ratio describes the relation between two amounts. It is the number of times one amount is contained in, or contains, the other.

1246. A ratio of 1.618 is called the golden ratio.

1247. The golden ratio has been used throughout history to design pleasing buildings, artworks, and music.

1248. The word geometry comes from the Greek words geo ("earth") and metria ("measure").

1249. A Greek mathematician named Euclid is called the father of geometry.

1250. Along with arithmetic, geometry was one of the two fields of early mathematics.

1251. Ancient Egyptians used geometry as far back as 3000 BC.

1252. The equals sign (=) was invented in 1557 by a Welsh mathematician named Robert Recorde.

1253. There are 293 ways to make change for $1 using pennies, nickels, dimes, quarters, and half dollars.

1254. The number 169 is equal to 132 and its reverse 961 is equal to 312.

1255. The Chinese were the first to use negative numbers around 2,200 years ago.

1256. The number –40 is the only number equal on both temperature scales.

1257. So, –40°C is equal to –40°F.

1258. In chess, there are 4,897,256 total possible positions after 5 moves by both players.

1259. There is a combination of 26,830 possible Tic-Tac-Toe games.

1260. The polar diameter of the Earth is approximately equal to half a billion inches.

1261. We use the base 10 or decimal number system.

1262. The Mayans counted by 20s, which is called a vigesimal system.

1263. The base two, or binary, system only uses the digits 0 and 1.

1264. Computers use the binary system to store data.

1265. The number 18 is the only one that is twice the sum of its digits. (18: 1 + 8 = 9: 9 × 2 = 18).

AWESOME OCEAN AND SEA FACTS

1267.   The Pacific is the world's largest ocean.

1268.   The Pacific covers 30 percent of the world's surface.

1269.   The Pacific is also the deepest ocean.

1270.   The average depth of the Pacific Ocean is 13,000 feet (4,000 meters).

1271.   The Pacific Ocean was named by Portuguese explorer Ferdinand Magellan.

1272.   Magellan called the ocean mar pacific, which means "peaceful sea."

1273.   Roughly 75 percent of the world's active volcanoes are located in the Ring of Fire in the Pacific Ocean.

1274.   The Ring of Fire has 90 percent of the world's earthquakes.

1275.   The Pacific is bordered by 55 countries.

1276.   The Pacific's Marianas Trench is the deepest ocean trench in the world.

1277.   The Marianas Trench is deeper than Mount Everest is tall.

1278.   The Pacific contains the second-largest island in the world, New Guinea.

1279.   There are more than 25,000 islands in the Pacific.

1280.   Most islands in the Pacific are located south of the Equator.

1281.   The Pacific has four types of islands.

1282.   They are continental islands, high islands, coral reefs, and lifted coral platforms.

1283.   Point Nemo in the Pacific Ocean is called a pole of inaccessibility. It is the farthest location from the ocean to the nearest coastline.

1284.   Point Nemo got its name from a character in Jules Verne's book 20,000 Leagues Under the Sea.

1285.   The world's largest spacecraft cemetery is located near Point Nemo.

1286.   There are more than 161 pieces of satellites and other spacecraft buried there.

1287.   Hydrothermal vents at the bottom of the ocean release water that can be as hot as 750°F (400°C).

1288.   The Atlantic is the second-largest ocean.

1289.   The Atlantic covers about 41 million square miles (106,190 square km).

1290. That's about 20 percent of the Earth's surface.

1291. This ocean gets its name from Atlas, a character in Greek mythology who holds up the world.

1292. The Atlantic was the first ocean to be crossed by ship.

1293. The Atlantic was also the first to be crossed by an airplane.

1294. The Mid-Atlantic Ridge is a mountain range underneath the Atlantic.

1295. The Mid-Atlantic Ridge is the longest mountain range on the planet.

1296. The Mid-Atlantic Ridge can be seen on satellite pictures.

1297. The deepest part of the Atlantic Ocean is the Milwaukee Deep, off the coast of Puerto Rico.

1298. The Milwaukee Deep is 27,493 feet (8,380 meters) deep.

1299. More rivers drain into the Atlantic than any other ocean.

1300. There are three types of islands in the Atlantic.

1301. They are pure oceanic islands, volcanic islands, and pure continental islands.

1302. The Atlantic is the saltiest ocean.

1303. Greenland, the largest island in the world, is located in the Atlantic.

1304. There is an underwater waterfall between Greenland and Iceland.

1305. The waterfall is formed by the temperature difference in the water on either side of the strait.

1306. Cold water from the east flows under warmer water from the west, creating a drop of 11,500 feet (3,505 meters).

1307. The Indian Ocean covers almost 20 percent of the Earth's surface.

1308. The Indian is the third-largest ocean.

1309. The Indian's average depth is 12,274 feet (3,741 meters).

1310. The Indian is the warmest ocean in the world.

1311. Because of its warmth, the Indian Ocean has less sea life than the Atlantic or Pacific Oceans.

1312. There is a submerged continent under the Indian Ocean.

1313. The submerged continent is called the Kerguelen Plateau.

1314. The Southern Ocean is also called the Antarctic Ocean because it surrounds Antarctica.

1315.   The Southern Ocean is the only ocean that goes all the way around the Earth.

1316.   Some scientists think the Southern Ocean doesn't really exist.

1317.   They say this ocean is actually part of the Indian, Pacific, and Atlantic Oceans.

1318.   The Southern Ocean ranges between 13,000 and 16,000 feet (4,000 and 5,000 meters) deep.

1319.   During the winter, about half of the Southern Ocean is covered by ice.

1320.   Many marine animals and birds live in the Southern Ocean.

1321.   The Arctic Ocean is the world's smallest ocean.

1322.   The Arctic is also the shallowest.

1323.   The Arctic Ocean is located around the North Pole.

1324.   It covers about 5,427,000 square miles (14,056,000 square km).

1325.   The Arctic's average depth is 3,406 feet (1,038 meters).

1326.   Its deepest point is Litke Deep, at 17,800 feet (5,450 meters).

1327.   Arctic comes from the Greek word arktos, which means "bear."

1328.   The Great Bear constellation appears just above the North Pole.

1329.   In 1896, Fridtjof Nansen became the first person to cross the Arctic Ocean by boat.

1330.   The Arctic can also be crossed by dog sled, as it freezes during the winter.

1331.   The Pacific is the world's most polluted ocean.

1332.   There are almost 2 trillion pieces of plastic floating in the Pacific.

1333.   Much of the plastic is located in several giant garbage patches.

1334.   Oceans can have lakes and rivers.

1335.   Seawater creates depressions on the ocean floor. Because the water around these depressions contains more salt than normal seawater, it sinks into the depressions, creating little lakes.

1336.   Some ocean lakes even have waves.

REPTILE AND AMPHIBIAN FACTS

1338. Crocodiles are related to dinosaurs.

1339. Some turtles can live more than 100 years.

1340. Reptiles are covered in scales or have a hard shell.

1341. Lizard and snake species make up the largest number of reptiles.

1342. Evidence of the first reptiles dates back to about 320 million years ago.

1343. There are four kinds of reptiles.

1344. They are turtles and tortoises, snakes and lizards, crocodilians, and tuataras.

1345. Crocodilians include crocodiles, alligators, caimans, and gharials.

1346. Tuataras only live on a few islands in New Zealand.

1347. Some reptiles shed their skin.

1348. Turtles and iguanas are the only reptiles that are herbivores.

1349. All other reptiles eat other animals.

1350. Most reptiles have a three-chambered heart.

1351. Crocodilians have a four-chambered heart.

1352. Amphibians have a two-chambered heart.

1353. Scientists think reptiles are an evolutionary stage between fish and amphibians and birds and mammals.

1354. Reptiles were the first land creatures to lay hard-shelled eggs.

1355. Crocodilians and some turtles lay a large number of eggs and bury them.

1356. The temperature outside the eggs determines whether the babies will be male or female.

1357. Usually, crocodilian eggs in very cold or very hot temperatures will hatch males.

1358. Crocodilian eggs in medium temperatures will hatch females.

1359. For turtles, cooler eggs hatch males and warmer eggs hatch females.

1360. Only boas and pythons give birth to live young.

1361. Young reptiles can survive on their own right after they are born.

1362. Some species of crocodiles swallow rocks so they can sink deeper under the water.

1363. Alligators and crocodiles can move very quickly when they are attacking prey.

1364. Snakes move by flexing muscles in their bodies.

1365. Many snakes are constrictors.

1366. Constrictors squeeze their prey so it can't breathe and then swallow the prey whole.

1367. If a snake eats a large meal, it can go weeks before it has to eat again.

1368. The largest turtle is the leatherback turtle.

1369. It can weigh up to 1,800 pounds (816 kg).

1370. The leatherback turtle's shell can be 8 feet (2.4 meters) long.

1371. The smallest reptile is the mini chameleon from Madagascar.

1372. This miniature reptile is only 1 inch (2.5 cm) long.

1373. The smallest snake is the thread snake at just 4 inches (10 cm) long.

1374. A spiny-tailed iguana can run up to 20 miles (32 km) per hour.

1375. The black mamba is the fastest snake.

1376. They can move up to 12.5 miles (20 km) per hour.

1377. Frogs can breathe through their lungs and also through their skin.

1378. Some snakes have more than 300 pairs of ribs.

1379. A turtle's shell is made of about 60 connected bones.

1380. Turtles have no ears, but they have excellent eyesight and sense of smell.

1381. Turtles can also feel vibrations from loud noises.

1382. Snakes and lizards smell with their tongues.

1383. Snakes have very poor hearing.

1384. Because snakes only have an inner ear, they can only detect vibrations through their jaws.

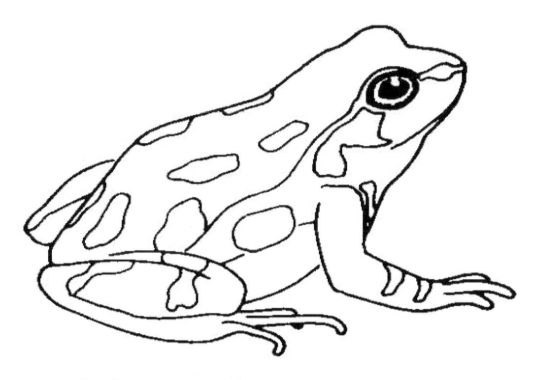

1385. Reptiles have a specialized chemically sensitive organ called the Jacobson's organ that can convert tastes into smells.

1386. Snakes also have a special organ that senses heat.

1387. Some snakes have these heat-seeking organs around their mouths.

1388. Pit vipers have them on either side of their heads.

1389. These organs can detect a temperature change as little as 2/1000 of a degree.

1390. This helps the snake detect and strike at prey even in complete darkness.

1391. Some species of lizards and iguanas have a third eye.

1392. This eye is located on top of the head and can only sense light and dark.

1393. Turtles can "feel" with their shells.

1394. Some turtles hibernate underwater.

1395. They "breathe" by absorbing air through thin skin around their butts.

1396. American alligators make such loud roars when they are looking for mates that they can be heard from miles away.

1397. Snakes and crocodilians are constantly losing and replacing teeth.

1398. Many times, these lost teeth are expelled through their droppings.

1399. Snakes and crocodilians have "backup" teeth that drop into place after a tooth has been lost.

1400. 6 Frogs swallow their food whole.

1401. Amphibians live the first part of their lives in the water.

1402. Their bodies change through metamorphosis so they can live on land.

1403. There are three types of amphibians: frogs and toads, newts and salamanders, and caecilians.

1404. Caecilians don't have legs and look a lot like snakes.

1405. Most amphibians live in or near water.

1406. Amphibian larvae eat plants, but adults are carnivores.

1407. Frogs cannot live in salt water.

1408. The word amphibian comes from the Greek amphibious, which means "two lives."

1409. A small cave salamander called the olm is the world's longest-lived amphibian.

1410. It can live for more than 100 years.

1411. Most amphibians only live for a year or two.

1412. Amphibians have excellent eyesight and can see in color.

PRESIDENTIAL FACTS

1414. John Adams was the first president to live in the White House.

1415. James Madison was the shortest president, at just 5 feet, 4 inches (1.63 meters) tall.

1416. Abraham Lincoln was the tallest. He was 6 feet, 4 inches (1.9 meters) tall.

1417. John Tyler had 15 children.

1418. Two of Tyler's grandchildren were still alive in the twentieth century.

1419. George Washington's false teeth were made of ivory, gold, and elephant and walrus tusks.

1420. James Buchanan was the only president who never married.

1421. Abraham Lincoln is honored in the Wrestling Hall of Fame.

1422. Ulysses S. Grant once got a ticket for speeding—on a horse!

1423. Rutherford B. Hayes was the first president to have a telephone.

1424. Hayes's phone number was 1.

1425. Benjamin Harrison had electricity installed in the White House.

1426. However, he was too afraid of it to touch the light switches.

1427. James Garfield could write Latin with one hand and Greek with the other at the same time.

1428. Abraham Lincoln was the first president to be assassinated.

1429. Grover Cleveland was the only president to be married in the White House.

1430. Cleveland is also the only president to serve two nonconsecutive terms.

1431. William Taft later served as a Supreme Court Justice.

1432. Taft swore in Presidents Calvin Coolidge and Herbert Hoover.

1433. There have been four presidential assassinations: Lincoln, Garfield, McKinley, and Kennedy.

1434. Theodore Roosevelt and Franklin D. Roosevelt were cousins.

1435. There have been two father-and-son presidential pairs: John and John Quincy Adams and George H.W. and George W. Bush.

1436. Calvin Coolidge's nickname was Silent Cal.

1437. Bill Clinton was the first president to hold an internet chat, in 1999.

1438. George H.W. Bush loved to wear colorful socks.

1439. James Madison was Princeton University's first graduate student.

1440. Monrovia, the capital of Liberia, is named after James Monroe.

1441. John Quincy Adams enjoyed skinny-dipping in the Potomac River.

1442. Andrew Jackson fought in more than 100 duels.

1443. James Buchanan regularly bought slaves in the South and brought them to Pennsylvania, where he set them free.

1444. Three presidents—Andrew Johnson, Bill Clinton, and Donald Trump—have been impeached by the House of Representatives.

1445. Nixon is the only president to resign from office.

1446. Gerald Ford, who replaced Nixon, was never actually elected to the presidency.

1447. Ronald Reagan was a successful movie actor before becoming president.

1448. While he was president, Grover Cleveland had a secret surgery to remove a cancerous tumor from his mouth.

1449. Theodore Roosevelt was shot while giving a speech. He continued speaking for 90 minutes.

1450. William Taft, the heaviest president, weighed 340 pounds (154 kg).

1451. James Madison was the lightest. He weighed 100 pounds (45 kg).

1452. Woodrow Wilson's face is on the $100,000 bill.

1453.   Herbert Hoover's son had two pet alligators that lived in the White House.

1454.   He also had an opossum.

1455.   Theodore Roosevelt had many unusual pets while he was president, including a pig, several bears, a badger, a snake named Emily Spinach, and a one-legged rooster.

1456.   Calvin Coolidge had a pet raccoon named Rebecca that walked on a leash.

1457.   Franklin Roosevelt was the only president to serve four terms.

1458.   Gerald Ford worked as a fashion model during college.

1459.   Several pro football teams wanted to draft Ford after he graduated from college.

1460.   Jimmy Carter once reported seeing a UFO.

1461.   Martin Van Buren was the first president born in the United States.

1462.   William Henry Harrison was only president for a month before dying of pneumonia.

1463.   Millard Fillmore and his wife established the first White House library.

1464.   Andrew Johnson came from a very poor family and never went to school.

1465.   His wife taught him to read and write.

1466.   The middle initial "S" in Ulysses S. Grant's and Harry S. Truman's names doesn't stand for anything.

1467. Rutherford B. Hayes started the traditional Easter Egg Roll on the White House lawn.

1468. Woodrow Wilson was the first president to give a speech over the radio.

1469. Franklin Roosevelt's radio broadcasts were called "Fireside Chats."

1470. Calvin Coolidge was born on the Fourth of July.

1471. Herbert Hoover was the first president born west of the Mississippi River.

1472. Lyndon Johnson is the only president to be sworn in on an airplane.

1473. He is also the only president sworn in by a woman.

1474. Ronald Reagan was the first divorced president.

1475.   Bill Clinton won two Grammy awards for spoken word recordings.

1476.   Jimmy Carter and Barack Obama have also won Grammys.

1477.   Theodore Roosevelt, Woodrow Wilson, Jimmy Carter, and Barack Obama have all won the Nobel Peace Prize.

1478.   Donald Trump is the first president who did not have a background in politics or the military.

1479.   Trump appeared in several movies and TV shows and starred in the reality show The Apprentice.

1480.   Eight presidents were left-handed.

1481.   They were James Garfield, Herbert Hoover, Harry Truman, Gerald Ford, Ronald Reagan, George H.W. Bush, Bill Clinton, and Barack Obama.

1482.   Only five presidents have had beards.

1483.   All were president during the nineteenth century.

1484.   Five presidents did not have biological children.

1485.   They were George Washington, James Madison, Andrew Jackson, James Polk, and James Buchanan.

1486.   Washington adopted his wife's two children from a previous marriage.

1487.   Five men became president without winning the popular vote: John Quincy Adams, Rutherford B. Hayes, Benjamin Harrison, George H.W. Bush, and Donald Trump.

1488.   Jimmy Carter became the longest living president in March 2019, at age 94 years, 172 days.

SUPER SPY FACTS

1490. During the 1960s, the CIA, a US spy agency, spent $15 million trying to use cats to spy on the Soviet Union.

1491. Shocker: It didn't work.

1492. During World War II, tiny cameras were attached to homing pigeons to film German military positions.

1493. In 1917, the Germans replaced a real tree with a fake one so a spy could hide inside.

1494. It took seven months for anyone to notice the tree was fake.

1495. Ian Fleming, the author of the James Bond novels, was himself a spy.

1496. James Bond was based on a real person who was a friend of Ian Fleming's.

1497. In 1963, Kim Philby, the head of British intelligence's anti-Soviet unit, was revealed as a Soviet spy.

1498. Philby escaped to the Soviet Union before he could be arrested.

1499. The cameras in spy satellites can photograph license plates from 50 miles (80 km) up in space.

1500. Paul Revere formed a spy ring called the Mechanics. The spies reported British troop movements.

1501. Confederate leader Jefferson Davis thought his dinner was being served by his slave, Little Mary. Little Mary was actually a spy who passed information back to the Union.

1502. The Culper Spy Ring was one of the largest spy operations in the American Revolution.

1503. One of the members of the Culper Spy Ring was a woman known only as 355.

1504. 355's identity remains unknown to this day.

1505. Spies often hide secret papers or radio transmitters in ordinary objects.

1506. These objects can include pipes, eyeglasses, and baseballs.

1507. In 1953, a boy delivering newspapers was paid with a hollow coin. Inside was a coded message. The coin turned out to be from a Russian spy.

1508. Spies often hide their true identity from their own family members.

1509. The US Navy has trained dolphins to locate and report underwater mines.

Printed in Great Britain
by Amazon